GII00835872

Ruth Illingworth has written extensively on aspects of Westmeath and Irish history. She has lectured at NUI Maynooth and belongs to the Women's Historical Association of Ireland. She is president of the Westmeath Historical and Archaeological Society and is a former Mayor of Mullingar. Her latest book is *A 1950s Irish Childhood* (The History Press).

Sheelagh called to the Northern Ireland Bar in November 1948

Sheelagh
Murnaghan
1924–1993
Stormont's only
Liberal MP

RUTH ILLINGWORTH

ULSTER HISTORICAL FOUNDATION

In Memory of
Dr Constance Rynder
1945–2017

FRONT COVER
Sheila Murnaghan © Victor Patterson

Published 2019
by Ulster Historical Foundation
www.ancestryireland.com
www.booksireland.org.uk

© Ruth Illingworth
ISBN 978-1-909556-73-7

DESIGN AND FORMATTING
FPM Publishing

COVER DESIGN
Dunbar Design

PRINTED IN THE EUROPEAN UNION

Contents

The Albert McElroy Memorial Fund

The Albert McElroy Memorial Fund was established to commemorate the life of Rev. Albert H. McElroy (1915–75) by promoting books on those subjects in which he was interested. The trustees of the fund (Berkley Farr, Jack Johnston, Allan Leonard, Ciaran McAteer and Rev. William McMillan) commissioned the Irish historian, Ruth Illingworth, to write this book about Sheelagh Murnaghan. They also organised the funding of the book through generous donations by sponsors, notably the Murnaghan family.

Acknowledgements

I WISH TO EXTEND MY GRATITUDE TO Sheelagh Murnaghan's sister, Lucille McGinley, and to her brother Tony Murnaghan for meeting me and sharing their memories of Sheelagh and permitting me to use family photographs and other material relating to her life.

I wish to thank Berkley and Mary Farr for their very kind hospitality providing me with so much information about Sheelagh as well as photographs. I particularly thank them and Dr Christopher Woods, for their proof reading and editing work. I also wish to thank Jack Johnston and Allan Leonard for all their help. Special thanks go to Sean Kelly, who first told me about Sheelagh's remarkable career and suggested that I should write this book.

I would like to thank the staff of the Linen Hall Library for their assistance. Thanks also to the staff at the Public Record Office of Northern Ireland (PRONI), Belfast Central Library, the National Library of Ireland and Westmeath County Library.

I also wish to thank Victor Patterson for permission to use his photograph of Sheelagh Murnaghan. Thanks also to Joe and Joan at Lir Business Centre, Mullingar for typing up the manuscript.

Lastly, I must express gratitude to the trustees of the Albert McElroy Memorial Fund and the sponsors whose subscriptions enabled the production of this book.

RUTH ILLINGWORTH
Mullingar, County Westmeath

Donors and Subscribers

Anthony Murnaghan
Colette Murnaghan
Lucille Murnaghan McGinley

Claire Murnaghan
David Murnaghan
Steve Murnaghan

David K. Alderdice
Professor, the Lord Alderdice
Lady Bloomfield
Duncan Brack
Stella Burnside
Rt Hon. Sir Vince Cable MP
Fionnuala Cook
Elizabeth Cowan
Rosemary Cowan
John Gaffikin-Cowan
Patrick Cross
Professor Brice Dickson
Berkley and Mary Farr
Stephen Farry MLA
Stewart Ferguson
Giles FitzHerbert
Meadhbh Keating Fitzpatrick
John Gray
John Hall
Kate Hall

Julia Harper
Dick Hunter
Jack Johnston
Sean and Roisin Kelly
Allan Leonard
Liberal Democrat History Group
Ciaran McAteer
Steve McBride
Michael Meadowcroft
Rev. William McMillan
Richard Moore (the late)
Mary Murnaghan
Anne Odling-Smee CBE
Robin Pennie
Rodney Smith
Michael Steed
Lord Steel of Aikwood
Professor Brian Walker
George Woodman
Dr C.J. Woods

Foreword

SHEELAGH MURNAGHAN PROVIDED Northern Ireland with a unique voice of reason and sanity in the years before and during the 'Troubles'. She was the only Liberal MP to be elected to the Stormont parliament, representing Queen's University from 1961 to 1969. In the face of Unionist opposition she attempted to introduce a Human Rights Bill on four occasions.

Sheelagh first came to public attention in the 1940s and 1950s on the hockey field where she played at an international level. After graduating in law at Queen's University she became the first woman to practise as a barrister in Northern Ireland. Her grandfather had been a Nationalist MP at Westminster, but Sheelagh was to join the recently revived Ulster Liberals led by Rev. Albert McElroy and she contested South Belfast in 1959. Their political platform offered a radical non-sectarian alternative to the electorate, at a time when peaceful constitutional change might have spared Northern Ireland much of the horror to come.

Throughout her time in Stormont and later, after her constituency was abolished, on various public bodies, Sheelagh was a person of the utmost integrity and a champion of those suffering injustice, even if it lost her support. Many of her causes such as human rights, proportional representation and the abolition of capital punishment were subsequently implemented long after she had first advocated them.

I was still a schoolboy when I attended my first Liberal meeting in August 1961 in Isibeal's Café in Belfast's Wellington Street. There were only half a dozen present but we approved Sheelagh's selection as candidate for the by-election at Queen's and it was a good night's work.

It is now over half a century since Sheelagh Murnaghan introduced her final Human Rights Bill at Stormont. We are aware too of the similar anniversary of the start of the Troubles. After 25 years since Sheelagh's death, it is timely to recall and recognise her contribution to Northern Ireland.

BERKLEY FARR
Former Ulster Liberal Party chairman

Introduction

'In Northern Ireland politics, I don't know which is the greatest
obstacle: to be a woman, a Catholic or a Liberal. I am all three.'

SHEELAGH MURNAGHAN[1]

NORTHERN IRELAND IN THE 1960s was a divided and unequal
society. Since its foundation forty years earlier only one party,
the Ulster Unionists, had held power. Some of the electorate had no
vote in local government elections as a result of archaic electoral laws,
long abandoned in the rest of the United Kingdom. Housing and jobs
could be allocated on the basis of religious affiliation rather than need
or ability. Catholics, who comprised nearly a third of the population
were largely absent from the highest levels of politics, the judiciary, the
civil service and academia. Women from all religious traditions were
also all but invisible in the public sphere of the deeply patriarchal
world of Northern Ireland in those days, as elsewhere. This male,
Protestant 'Wee Province' was a world in which the tribal voices of
Unionist/British and Nationalist/Irish all but drowned out other
voices – the voices of those who wished to live a life not defined by
religious affiliation or loyalty to the Union Jack or Tricolour.

Into this world came Sheelagh Murnaghan from Omagh, County
Tyrone; a Catholic; a woman; a member of the Liberal Party. For just
over seven years she was the Ulster Liberal Party's only member of the
Stormont Parliament. She was one of just three women in that
parliament. She was a Catholic who was comfortable with Northern
Ireland's membership of the United Kingdom and saw Northern
Ireland as a distinctive part of the island of Ireland with its own
identity and culture.

Sheelagh Murnaghan loved her country and wanted Northern
Ireland to look good to the rest of the world, but she saw very clearly

all that was wrong and rotten in the province. A lawyer by profession, she focused her forensic legal training and skill on the ways in which the state denied equality of opportunity to a third of its citizens. Unlike so many in public life, she did not rant or roar. Instead she spoke quietly but firmly about the 'disadvantage' experienced by so many and about the fact that in Northern Ireland of the 1960s, there were 'degrees of citizenship'. Discrimination was something 'to be angry about'.

To remedy the ills in Northern Ireland society, Sheelagh Murnaghan brought before the Stormont parliament a Human Rights Bill. This was the first time such a bill had ever been presented in any British or Irish legislature. Drawing on American and Canadian legislation, her bill was aimed at ending the evil of discrimination by making discrimination on grounds of creed, colour, gender or political views illegal and setting up a Human Rights Commission which could provide legal remedy for those who believed themselves to be the victims of discrimination.

Four times she brought forward her pioneering legislation and four times the government rejected her proposals. The history of the late twentieth century in Northern Ireland might have been a very different one had her bill been accepted.

Sheelagh Murnaghan was an eloquent voice for the Traveller/Itinerant community too. In parliament she harried ministers constantly over the appalling way in which that most marginalised community was treated. She helped set up a school for Traveller children and visited their campsites. There was absolutely no political gain to be made by such actions, but that never deterred her. Sheelagh Murnaghan was a genuine liberal and her belief in equality was absolute.

Throughout her life, she was used to being a lone woman in a man's world. Brought up to believe herself equal to men, she fought to ensure equality for women in the workplace. Half a decade before laws requiring equal pay were enacted, she was seeking an end to the situation in which women were paid less for doing exactly the same job as men. In 1983, she adjudicated the first case of sexual harassment ever brought in the United Kingdom. The ruling she gave in that case influenced courts in Britain, Ireland and the rest of the European Union.

By any standards, Sheelagh Murnaghan was a remarkable person. She was the first female barrister to practise in Northern Ireland; a talented sportswoman who played hockey for Ulster and Ireland; the only Liberal Party MP in the 50-year history of the Northern Ireland Parliament. In a country riven by sectarianism, she was consistently a voice of reason and humanity, endlessly challenging the widely held assumption that it was normal and right to 'look after one's own people' and 'do down the other side'. A patriot in the most genuine meaning of the word she tried to save her country from its demons. Her efforts were rejected and Northern Ireland paid a terrible price for that rejection.

Most of the reforms which Sheelagh Murnaghan sought to introduce into Northern Ireland are now in place. She did not live to see the end of the conflict which she had tried so hard to prevent, but it may be said that the 1998 Good Friday/Belfast Agreement embodied much of what she wished to achieve. Half a century after her fourth and final Human Rights Bill was debated, and a quarter of a century after her death, it is time to remember Sheelagh Murnaghan OBE, lawyer, politician, human rights activist and sportswoman, by bringing her into the light of history.

Notes

1   Quoted by Jeremy Thorpe in a letter to *The Times*, 22 Sep. 1993.

Sheelagh as a child in her grandfather's house, Lisanelly

1

Childhood

SHEELAGH MARY MURNAGHAN WAS BORN in Omagh, County Tyrone, on 26 May 1924. Her father, Vincent Murnaghan, was town surveyor for Omagh and Strabane, and Assistant County Surveyor for County Tyrone from 1922 until 1964.[1] Her mother, Ann Morrogh, was from a County Cork business family and was the niece of an Irish Home Rule MP, John Morrogh, who had worked in South Africa for years, before returning to Ireland to set up a woollen factory. She and Vincent met while they were studying at University College Dublin (UCD).[2]

The Murnaghan family were deeply involved in politics, the law and science, and had a remarkable range of achievements to which Sheelagh would make her own later contribution.

Sheelagh's grandfather, George Murnaghan, was born in County Down in 1847 and emigrated to the USA where he was successful in business. Returning to Ireland, he settled in Omagh and became involved in politics, serving as Irish Nationalist MP for Mid-Tyrone from 1895 to 1910. He also served on Omagh Rural District Council and Tyrone County Council for many years.[3]

In the aftermath of the 1916 Easter Rising, the British government was prepared to grant immediate Home Rule to Ireland providing that the six Ulster counties with Protestant majorities were excluded. A meeting of the Home Rule Party in Belfast endorsed the idea of temporary exclusion. George Murnaghan and his solicitor son, George Jnr, were among those who opposed the idea of exclusion. George Murnaghan Snr acted as 'an éminence grise' to a group of younger Irish nationalists – including George Jnr, who drew up a document, later known as 'The Omagh Remonstrance', which rejected any form of exclusion, however temporary. In July 1916, George Jnr was one of the founding members of a new Nationalist party, the Irish Nation League, sometimes known as 'The League of the Seven Attorneys' due to the number of lawyers involved. The Irish Nation League was absorbed into Sinn Féin the following year.[4] During the War of Irish Independence (1919–21), George Murnaghan Snr acted as an advisor to Arthur Griffith and other senior Sinn Féin figures on Ulster issues.[5] Along with his Nationalist colleagues, he refused to recognise the new Northern Ireland administration created in 1921, and continued to give allegiance to the new Dáil Éireann government in Dublin instead. Like most Irish Nationalists in Northern Ireland, he supported the Anglo-Irish Treaty. Retiring from politics in 1924, George Murnaghan died at his Omagh home on 13 January 1929.[6]

James Murnaghan, one of Sheelagh's uncles, was a major figure in the Irish legal profession for many decades. Born in the USA, he attended University College Dublin, where his friends included James Joyce. Together with Joyce and a future Supreme Court Judge, Hugh Kennedy, Murnaghan was a contributor to the student magazine *St. Stephen's*. He remained on friendly terms with Joyce and would later visit him in Paris. Called to the Irish Bar in 1903, he practised in the Northern and Midland circuits. In 1919, he represented Pope Benedict XV in a court case arising out of the will of an Athlone businessman who had bequeathed £10,000 to the Pope.[7] Murnaghan also worked in academia, as professor of Jurisprudence, Roman Law and International Law at UCD. In 1922, James Murnaghan served as a member of the committee appointed by the provisional government of the Irish Free State to draw up a constitution for the new state.

In 1924, when the new Irish Courts Service came into being, he was appointed to the High Court. A year later he was appointed to the Supreme Court, on which he would serve for 28 years. One of his first judgements was a ruling which interpreted Article One of the 1921 Anglo-Irish Treaty as making 'Southern Ireland' an independent State. Interestingly, in the light of his niece Sheelagh's later opposition to internment without trial and to the Special Powers Act in Northern Ireland, Judge Murnaghan upheld the constitutionality of special military tribunals to deal with subversives in the Irish Free State in 1934, and the Offences Against the State Act of 1939, which permitted internment. Judge Murnaghan retired from the courts in 1953. A noted art connoisseur, he was a member of the board of the National Gallery of Ireland. He died in Dublin in 1973, at the age of 92.[8]

Francis Dominic Murnaghan, another of Sheelagh's uncles, made his name as a leading mathematician of twentieth-century America. Having received a first class honours degree from UCD in 1913, he went to the United States in 1914, where he took a PhD at Johns Hopkins University, Baltimore. Most of his career was spent at Johns Hopkins, where he was professor of mathematics from 1928 to 1948. During a year as a visiting professor at the Princeton Institution for Advanced Study in 1936, he worked with Albert Einstein and John von Neumann. He also held visiting professorships at the Dublin Institute for Advanced Studies in 1948 and 1957, and worked in São Paulo, Brazil in the 1950s, making a major contribution to maths teaching there. His research output resulted in 15 books and 90 research papers, including the definitive reference work in the field of Hydrodynamic Theory and the Murnaghan-Nakayama formula for calculating character values for symmetric groups. He edited the *American Journal of Mathematics* from 1930 to 1948. Throughout his life he retained a love of Ireland and an Irish accent. He died in 1976.[9] His son, Frank Murnaghan became a distinguished lawyer and a strong influence on Sheelagh.

Yet another distinguished relative of Sheelagh's was her cousin, Maurice Murnaghan, the son of her uncle Daniel, a graduate of UCD Medical School, where he won gold medals and other awards. Maurice lectured at UCD in anatomy, pharmacology and therapeutics from 1942 to 1948. From 1948 to 1964, he worked in Canada, serving as professor of pharmacology at Ottawa University and as Deputy Registrar of the Medical Council of Canada, as well as President of the Pharmacology Society of Canada. On his return to Ireland in 1964 he became a professor of Physiology at UCD. He was elected a member of the Royal Irish Academy in 1970 and was President of the biological sciences section of the Royal Academy of Medicine. He died in 1982.[10]

Another cousin of Sheelagh's was Judge George Murnaghan, who served on the Irish High Court from 1954 to 1979. The television broadcaster Dermot Murnaghan is her nephew.

Sheelagh spent most of her childhood in Omagh, the county town of Tyrone. She was the eldest of a family of eight and throughout her life, she would be the one whom her siblings looked up to.[11]

Omagh was a quiet town where the two communities – Catholic and Protestant – generally got along well. Susan McKay would later describe

Omagh as a 'mild, mannerly place'.[12] During her childhood, Sheelagh had as many Protestant friends as Catholic ones, and her parents were comfortably part of the town's middle class.[13]

Sheelagh never regarded herself as a feminist, but she did believe in equality. Her parents treated their sons and daughters equally and Sheelagh was always able to take it for granted that she could follow whatever career she wanted. In what would prove to be a preparation for her political career, she was encouraged by her father to take part in debates around the family dinner table. Vincent Murnaghan would throw in a topic for discussion and the debate could sometimes get quite hot and heavy.[14] Sheelagh's interest in and talent for sport may have come from her mother, who played tennis and badminton.

Sheelagh attended the Loreto School in Omagh. The Loreto Order, founded in 1609 by Mary Ward, who angered the Church hierarchy for stating that 'One day women will amount to much', had an ethos which encouraged their pupils to treat all people with respect and tolerance and to use their talents in the service of the wider community in whichever career they chose to follow.[15]

The outbreak of the Second World War brought disruption to the Murnaghan household. The family home, Lisanelly House, was taken over by the army and the family moved to Dublin for a time, where Sheelagh attended Loreto Abbey, Rathfarnham (where Mother Theresa of Calcutta had studied English a few years earlier). On their return to Omagh, the Murnaghans lived for a while over the business premises they owned before moving to a new house – Belview. Lisanelly remained in military possession until the early twenty-first century.[16]

Notes

1   *Ulster Herald*, 14 Nov. 1964.
2   Interview with Lucille McGinley (sister of Sheelagh), 2 Aug. 2017.
3   James Maguire and James Quinn (eds), *Dictionary of Irish Biography* (Cambridge, 2009), vol. 6, p. 787.
4   Eamon Phoenix, *Northern Nationalism* (Belfast, 1994), p. 24.
5   *DIB*, vol. 6, p. 787.
6   Ibid.
7   *Westmeath Independent*, 12 Apr. 1919.

8   *DIB*, vol. 6, p. 788.
9   Ibid., pp 786–7.
10 Ibid., p. 790.
11 *Ulster Herald*, 23 Sep. 1993.
12 *Magill*, Sep. 1998.
13 Interview with Lucille McGinley, 2 Aug. 2017.
14 Interview with Tony Murnaghan (brother of Sheelagh), June 2017.
15 https://loreto.ie/history/mary-ward, accessed 14 May 2019.
16 Interview with Lucille McGinley, 2 Aug. 2017.

Sheelagh as a student

2

Student, Lawyer and Sports Star

In 1943, SHEELAGH COMPLETED HER SECONDARY education and moved on to university. While there was a family tradition of attending UCD, she went instead to Queen's University Belfast. The war was still on and she came to a city where the blackout was in force at night and in which many areas were in ruins following the massive air raids of 1941. Train and bus journeys between Omagh and Belfast were long and tedious because of fuel shortages. However, Sheelagh enjoyed herself in college. She began an arts degree but switched to law at the end of her first year – following in the footsteps of her uncles James and George.[1]

Queen's was then a largely Protestant and Unionist institution with far more male than female students and lecturers. It was Sheelagh's first encounter with 'a man's world' – one which she would experience many times throughout her life, and it was also her first experience of life in a Unionist/Protestant majority community.

She worked hard at her studies and also took part in the social and sporting life of the university. She was the first woman to be elected as the president of the University's Literary and Scientific Debating Society – the Literific – in 1946. At this stage she had little interest in politics – apart from being involved in closing down the University's Russian Society. In 1948, she was called to the Northern Ireland Bar – becoming one of the first female barristers in Northern Ireland and, for many years, the only practising woman barrister in the country. Perhaps because of her gender, she found it hard to get work in the courts. Throughout her legal career she would be employed in writing up cases for the Northern Ireland law reports. In 1953, she compiled a table of all cases and consolidated index of every court case heard in Northern Ireland since 1925.[2]

19 50,

FAST TELEGRAPH, WEDNESDAY, MAY 3

Ulster members of the Irish Women's Hockey team, before leaving Belfast to play in the World Triennial Hockey Tournament in Johannesburg, South Africa. Matches will be played against England, Scotland, U.S. and South Africa. Left to right—Miss Sheilagh Murnaghan, Miss Mary Bell, Mrs. S. Hayes (Umpire), Miss Kathleen Pender, Miss L. Taylor.

Departure for the World Triennial Hockey
Tournament in Johannesburg, 1950

During the 1940s and 1950s, Sheelagh made a name for herself nationally and internationally, as a hockey player, playing for Instonians, Ulster and Ireland. In the 1955–6 and 1957–8 seasons, she captained the Ireland team. Reporters described her as 'a diminutive but ferocious fullback'. On 9 March 1957, she was part of the Ireland team which played against England in Wembley Stadium in front of television cameras and almost 50,000 (mostly English) cheering schoolgirls.[3] England won but the English papers praised the skill and tenacity of the whole Irish team and considered them unlucky not to have won.

A year later, Sheelagh captained Ireland to a 2–2 draw against England in Belfast. The reporter wrote that; 'the entire Irish team is deserving of congratulations for an inspiring performance'.[4] In a match against Scotland in March 1958, which resulted in a 1–1 draw, it was reported that Sheelagh was 'prominent amongst the Irish defence, always giving the impression of extreme calm.'[5]

In 1950, Sheelagh toured South Africa with the Ireland team. She visited the United States with the Irish players in 1954 and was again there as a coach in 1958. On the latter occasions she made the acquaintance of her American relatives. She came to love America and was deeply interested in Democrat politics and in the developing civil rights movement.[6] In years to come, she would look to American legislation as a blueprint for her own human rights legislative proposals for Northern Ireland. As Constance Rynder noted: 'These early contacts – kept fresh by subsequent encounters in the USA and Ireland – would play a significant role in nurturing her political and legal philosophy.'[7]

By the late fifties, Sheelagh was moving towards a political career. Given that both her paternal grandfather and a maternal great-uncle had been members of parliament; this was not perhaps surprising in a country where political dynasties are common. But Sheelagh parted company with the Irish Nationalist ideology of the Murnaghans. Instead she joined a newly established political party – the Ulster Liberal Association.

Notes

1   Interview with Lucille McGinley, 2 Aug. 2017.
2   Published as *Consolidated Table of Cases Reported and Consolidated Index Summary 1925–1953*.
3   *Hockey Field*, vol. 44, no. 14, 16 Apr. 1957, pp 974–5.
4   Ibid., no. 15, 12 Apr. 1958, p. 290.
5   Ibid., p. 292.
6   Interview with Lucille McGinley, 2 Aug. 2017.
7   Constance Rynder, 'Sheelagh Murnaghan and the Struggle for Human Rights in Northern Ireland', *Irish Studies Review*, vol. 14, no. 4 (2006), p. 447.

1963 Liberal Assembly in Brighton: Kina Lubbock, Eric Lubbock MP
(Orpington), Richard Moore, Chris Woods, Berkley Farr, Sean Kelly,
Bob Huston, Albert McElroy and Sheelagh Murnaghan MP

3

The Ulster Liberals

THE LIBERAL PARTY HAD ONCE BEEN STRONGLY represented in Ireland – winning 66 seats in the 1868 General Election.[1] The Liberal Party in Ireland drew its support from both Catholics and Protestants. However, the rise of the Irish Home Rule movement from the 1870s onwards drew Roman Catholic voters away from liberalism, and the Liberal Party's support for Home Rule from the 1880s cost it Protestant support, leading to the party's rapid decline in Ireland. Despite this it still returned MPs until 1918. Following the creation of Northern Ireland, the Liberals ran candidates in the 1929 Northern Irish and United Kingdom general elections. In the Westminster elections, the Liberals in Northern Ireland won 17 per cent of the vote and in the elections to the local parliament, their five candidates won almost of one third of the vote.[2] However, the first past the post system, reintroduced by the Unionist government, meant that they failed to win any seats. After 1929, the party disappeared for more than a quarter of a century.

In March 1956, a meeting took place in Belfast which resulted in the setting up of a new autonomous Ulster Liberal Association for Northern Ireland – later renamed The Ulster Liberal Party.[3] The first chairman of the party was Albert McElroy. Albert was born in Scotland in 1915 to parents originally from Ulster. When he was 15, his family moved to Northern Ireland. He attended Trinity College Dublin and served in the British Army during the Second World War. He was ordained in 1954 as a minister of the Non-Subscribing Presbyterian Church of Ireland, which is Unitarian in tendency. He was its Moderator from 1967 to 1969. Originally McElroy had been a socialist, and stood for the Northern Ireland Labour Party in the 1945 Northern Irish and 1950 and 1951 UK general elections.

Gradually, however his political opinions shifted towards liberalism. While accepting that Northern Ireland would remain British until the majority of its people decided otherwise, he himself believed that Ireland would one day be reunited and was proud of the 'Radical and Liberal tradition' of the Ulster Presbyterians and their role in the United Irishmen of the 1790s and America's independence struggle. He was also proud of the Liberal Party's support for Irish Home Rule. McElroy's ambition was to offer the voters of Northern Ireland an alternative to the tribal politics of Unionism and Nationalism.[4]

The Ulster Liberals got their first chance to win votes in 1958 when a general election for the Stormont parliament took place. Albert McElroy stood for the Queen's University constituency. This was the only constituency in which proportional representation was still used, returning four MPs. The electorate consisted of the graduates of the university. It was a more middle class, educated and possibly less polarised electorate than elsewhere. As one of the six candidates running, McElroy received 13 per cent of the first preference vote and came in third place, but the second preference votes of the Unionist candidates meant that he failed to be elected. Nevertheless, the support he received indicated that there was a market in Northern Irish politics for liberalism.[5]

In October 1959, a UK general election was held. A meeting took place to choose a Liberal candidate for the South Belfast constituency. Sheelagh Murnaghan, who had joined the party just a few months earlier, was selected as the candidate. As she would recall, Albert McElroy asked her to be the candidate ('I did not want to be rude to the clergyman').[6] In her election literature, Sheelagh urged the electors to turn away from the sectarian politics and vote for something new:

> It is the realisation of the dire need for a fresh approach to politics which has given rise to the formation of the new Ulster Liberal Association composed of members from all sections of the community. Our aim is to encourage the people of Northern Ireland, irrespective of creed or social class, to get together for the common good.[7]

The question as to where the Liberals stood on Northern Ireland's constitutional position was not one which could be evaded. Sheelagh's grandfather and uncle had been strong Irish Nationalists who had campaigned fiercely against partition and never forgave Liberal prime minister David Lloyd George for abandoning northern Catholics in 1921 to a Protestant state. Sheelagh's own views were rather different, as her election address showed.

> Ulster Liberals are free to hold their own individual opinions on this issue but are pledged to maintain Northern Ireland's constitutional position unless the majority of the people desire to revise it. For my part, I do not accept that the reunification of Ireland is something which can never happen, but I am absolutely opposed to any attempt to force the people of Northern Ireland into the Republic against their will.[8]

During the election campaign, the voters of South Belfast were treated to the unique sight of a Protestant minister (McElroy) canvassing with a Catholic woman; in appearance he was plump while she was petite. It was certainly an example of new politics in action – the very 'personification of the non-sectarian and progressive message that the Liberals were putting forward.' Not everyone was able to accept that message, as the Rev. McElroy would later comment: 'It's amazing the way folk can get mixed up. To Nationalist diehards Sheelagh Murnaghan is a disguised Unionist; Unionists regard me as disguised Republican.'

The Belfast election campaign was followed across in Britain by the UK Liberal Party. *Liberal News* described Sheelagh 'as the bravest Liberal candidate among all the 11 score running in this election' and 'a gallant fighter for social unity in a land of sterile conflict'. When the election took place, Sheelagh performed poorly, securing only 7.5 per cent of the vote. The winning Unionist candidate got 70 per cent of the vote and the bulk of what could be called the 'cross community' vote went to the Northern Ireland Labour Party.[9]

In 1961 another chance arose for the Liberals, when a by-election was called for the Queen's University constituency following the death of the Unionist MP. Sheelagh was selected as the candidate at a meeting in August, 'attended by just 7 people.' It was a straight contest against the Unionist candidate, Dr Samuel Rodgers. The election aroused great interest in the Omagh area, with several local Queen's graduates stating that 'they were making a special point of sending in their ballots on this occasion. They intended, they say, to vote for Miss Murnaghan.'[10]

1962 Stormont election: Albert McElroy (Ards), Arthur Burns
(North Down) and Sheelagh Murnaghan (Queen's University)

The sixties had begun and in Northern Ireland, as elsewhere, there
was a sense of change in the air. In her election addresses, Sheelagh
caught that mood. 'If we cannot immediately have a government
which is prepared to lift its head out of the sand and focus on the
second half of the twentieth century, at least we must put some people
in parliament who would try to jolt it into some sort of recognition of
the needs of our time.'[11]

Election Day was 22 November 1961, and the voter turnout was
45.1 per cent. When the votes were counted, the Liberals had 2,622
votes to the Unionists 2,370. Sheelagh Murnaghan was now a
member of the Northern Ireland Parliament.[12]

Albert McElroy was 'almost apoplectic with excitement' and, after
the declaration of the result, he went out and bought packets of fish
and chips for the Liberal supporters and their new MP.[13] Sheelagh's
election was a great boost for the Liberals. It was the first time since
its formation that a Liberal had been elected in Northern Ireland.
Over the next year party membership increased and new Liberal
associations were formed across the province. As McElroy later
remarked: 'Before Miss Murnaghan won that Queen's seat for us the
word liberal, either with a small or capital L was dirty, now they all
want to be liberals but in the long run the only thing that matters is
that liberal ideas and principles are achieved.'[14]

Sheelagh's election also had a wider significance, as the *Ulster Herald* noted; 'It also confirmed the trend in British politics – that towards the revival of Liberalism as a traditional alternative to Toryism.'[15] The Queen's by-election result was another step in a national rise in support for the Liberal Party. This followed on from the by-election win at Torrington in 1958 by Mark Bonham-Carter and the election of Jeremy Thorpe in North Devon in the 1959 general election. Just four months after Sheelagh's victory, the Liberals in Britain won a sensational by-election victory in Orpington when Eric Lubbock captured what had been a safe Conservative seat.

Sheelagh's election meant that the Liberals now had a voice in Northern Ireland's parliament to promote Liberalism and to challenge the Unionist-dominated government, and, in Sheelagh, the party 'had acquired both a courageous and colourful operator.'

Notes

1   Gordon Gillespie, 'The Ulster Liberal Party 1956–1973', MSSc thesis (Queen's University Belfast, 1984), p. 4.
2   Ibid., p. 5.
3   Ibid., p. 10.
4   Gordon Gillespie, *Albert McElroy: The Radical Minister 1915–1975* (Belfast, 1985), p. 11.
5   Gordon Gillespie, 'The Ulster Liberal Party', p. 17.
6   Constance Rynder, 'Sheelagh Murnaghan and the Struggle for Human Rights', *Journal of Liberal History*, no. 71 (Summer 2011), p. 14.
7   Gordon Gillespie, 'The Ulster Liberal Party', p. 14.
8   Berkley Farr, 'Liberalism in Unionist Northern Ireland', *Journal of Liberal Democrat History*, no. 33 (Winter 2001–02), p. 29.
9   *Ulster Herald*, 17 Nov. 1961.
10 Gillespie, *Ulster Liberal Party*, p. 25.
11 Ibid., p. 25.
12 Gillespie, *Albert McElroy*, p. 21.
13 Ibid., p. 21.
14 *Ulster Herald*, 2 Dec. 1961.
15 Ibid.

1970 UK general election:
Major Hamilton Simmonds-Gooding (N. Down), Richard Moore (N. Antrim),
Albert McElroy, Sheelagh Murnaghan, John Quinn (S. Down)

4

The Honourable and Learned Member

ON HER ELECTION, SHEELAGH MURNAGHAN FOUND herself once more entering 'a man's world.' She was one of just three women in the 52-member Stormont House of Commons and one of only 11 women (nine MPs and two Senators) ever elected to the Parliament during its 51-year existence.[1] She was not, however, in any way intimidated by the virtually all-male environment. She was happy to join the men in the bar for brandy and cheroots. There were no ladies' toilets on the business floor of Stormont, so she used the men's facilities. On one occasion she persuaded the Attorney-General of Northern Ireland, Basil Kelly, to stand guard outside for her.[2]

Her earthy sense of humour and no-nonsense style gained her the respect of the men and she made friends across the political spectrum. In the years to come, however, she would challenge the cosy world of Northern Ireland's patriarchal and Protestant establishment.

She took her seat at Stormont the week after her election – 'a parliamentary party complete in herself', as the *Ulster Herald* noted.[3] The Unionist MP Phelim O'Neill gave her a warm and witty welcome to parliament.

> Her appearance in this chamber, as a Liberal, although not quite as rare as the reappearance of the great auk, is at least as uncommon as the appearance among us of the golden aureole or the hoopae. I wonder very much whether it is some strange current or eddy in the upper atmosphere of migration that has brought her here or whether it is a genuine extension in the advance of the species.[4]

In keeping with parliamentary traditions, Sheelagh's maiden speech was uncontroversial; reflecting her sporting interests and experience she spoke about the subject of rate relief for sports clubs. She expressed her concern that high rates would drive many small sports clubs out of existence, particularly hockey clubs where the membership was drawn from the ranks of working women.[5]

Her first parliamentary question was addressed to the Prime Minister, Lord Brookeborough. Since 1956, the Irish Republican Army (IRA) had been waging a military campaign in the border areas, which had claimed the lives of a number of police officers and IRA volunteers. The Irish government had brought in internment and military tribunals to deal with the crisis and the Northern government was also using emergency powers. In her question to Brookeborough, Sheelagh asked whether he would:

> Make a request to the Taoiseach of the Republic to consider a temporary scheme whereby an area of approximately five miles on either side of the border would be patrolled jointly by the RUC and Civic Guards in order to ensure complete freedom of movement for patrols in the area and with a view to demonstrating beyond question that both sides are agreed in their determination to put an end to IRA activities and that they are prepared to co-operate in full for the purpose.[6]

Brookeborough's written reply was that he 'could not accept her suggestion'. The idea of joint RUC/Gardaí patrols in the border region would be one which Sheelagh would raise again a decade later.

Just six months after her election, Sheelagh had to face the voters again when a general election for Northern Ireland was called. A Liberal Association had been formed at Queen's University in March 1962 and members of this branch were able to give Sheelagh assistance during the election campaign, putting up posters, posting letters and organising transport for Sheelagh and the other three Liberal candidates.[7]

In her election address Sheelagh referred to the significance of her by-election victory and referred with unjustified modesty to her own political abilities:

> You struck a blow for freedom of thought and better understanding among our people. The result of that by-election opened up new horizons in Northern Ireland. I only wish that I did not feel so very inadequate as a politician. However, I hope to improve with experience if you see fit to give me the opportunity.[8]

Sheelagh was re-elected comfortably, on the first count with 1,698 votes – 25 per cent of the total poll. The other three Liberal candidates failed to be elected – although Albert McElroy took nearly a third of the vote in Ards and Arthur Burns got a similar percentage of the vote in North Down. Another Queen's graduate, Judith Rosenfield, did badly in the Belfast Ballynafeigh seat because the anti-Unionist vote was split. In August, the Liberals won their first local council seat when Brian Wimpress was elected in Bangor.[9]

Back at Stormont, Sheelagh resumed her role as the standard bearer for the Liberal Party and their values. There was a housing shortage in Northern Ireland, with thousands on waiting lists for houses and many living in sub-standard accommodation. Sheelagh asked for an increased house building programme. The slowness and caution of the government and civil service on the matter annoyed her:

> I should like to see a little bit more of the American type of approach which says that 'this has to be done, there is such an obstacle, how do we get round it?' We could do with a lot more of that type of approach which does not regard obstacles as something which are permanent/impediments. This government's approach is that there is this, that and the other obstacles and consequently there is nothing which can be done about it.[10]

The IRA Border Campaign had ended in February 1962 and the state of emergency was lifted. A few months later the Belfast Republican Labour MP, Harry Diamond, tabled a motion calling for the release of prisoners detained during the emergency. Sheelagh supported this, telling the house:

> I hope the minister will give consideration to this matter for the sake of humanity and the impact it could have on public opinion in counteracting the view that this State is not conducted according to ordinary, civilised modern behaviour. By forgiving those who have trespassed against us I believe we would score high marks for Northern Ireland across the world.[11]

The Liberals favoured the highest degree of co-operation between Northern Ireland and the Republic and Sheelagh spoke in favour of such co-operation during a Stormont debate in March 1963. She was impatient with those politicians who kept their eyes fixed firmly on the past and constantly revisited old grievances. 'As is usual when there is any subject which bears in any way on the Border, we have wandered again down the by-ways of history, in fact some of these by-ways might be described as spiked roads.'[12] Welcoming the more pragmatic approach to Northern Ireland taken by Taoiseach Seán Lemass, Sheelagh stated:

> I think it is time that the Republic did, in fact, recognise officially the position which they at the moment recognise 'de facto' – the position that there are two parliaments in Ireland. The fact that we have two separated political positions and administration is absolutely no reason for foregoing economic co-operation which would benefit both sides.[13]

When the veteran Nationalist and Anti-Partition MP Cahir Healy intervened to state that Ireland was 'One Nation', Sheelagh retorted: 'Of course Ireland is one nation. We are all Irish but that is no reason whatever why we should not have separate political administration if it so suits us.'[14] Criticising those Unionists who opposed closer co-operation across the border, Sheelagh raised an issue which she would return to many times during her political career – her desire to see Northern Ireland having a good standing in the world and her concern that the attitudes and behaviour of those in power damaged the country's reputation. 'The discouragement of co-operation brings us a certain amount of contempt and scorn. It would do us a great deal of good indeed in the eyes of the outside world if there were to be – on our side – a gesture of friendship from the North towards the South.'[15] Commenting on those whose mindset remained stuck in a time warp, she declared:

> Let us look ahead to where we are going from here and let us not worry quite so much about the interminable arguments and disagreements as to who was to blame, who was in the right or who was in the wrong. Let us move on to something upon which we can get agreement and let us look to the future.[16]

Unemployment in Northern Ireland was rising as industrial decline set in during the 1960s. Sheelagh supported the idea of individuals being able to invest in industrial start-ups as a way of creating new employment. The Liberals supported co-operation between workers and management and the idea of co-operative enterprises. Again, Sheelagh voiced her impatience with those who clung to ideological prejudices: 'Let us agree to put our backs into the job and offer the province a bit of hope for the future.'[17]

With jobs at Shorts aircraft factory (one of Northern Ireland's biggest employers) under threat, Sheelagh was part of a delegation that went to London in July 1963 to meet with government ministers responsible for defence.

In January 1963, there was a major controversy when the Northern Ireland government's representative in London (the Ulster Agent as he was known) refused, on the government's instructions, to meet a trade union delegation from Belfast because it included the Northern committee of the Dublin-based Irish Congress of Trade Unions (ICTU). During a debate on a motion censuring the Ulster Agent, Sheelagh launched a fierce attack on what she described as 'the so-called government which we have here. They are hag-ridden by terrors of really I know not what.'[18]

As usual, the issue of Northern Ireland's constitutional status got dragged into the debate, which Sheelagh angrily denounced:

> To drag in the constitution as a red herring is typical of what we have had to suffer here for many years. If this one plank on which the government seem able to get support in the country continues to be dragged out to cut across the vital interests of any section of the Northern Ireland community then something will have to be done about it.[19]

In March 1963, Lord Brookeborough finally retired after 20 years as Northern Ireland prime minister. His successor was Terence O'Neill, who was on the modernising wing of the Unionist Party. He gradually began to reach out to the Catholic community – visiting a Catholic school, meeting senior Catholic clergy. In January 1965, he invited Irish premier Seán Lemass to Belfast and met him at Stormont. A parliamentary debate took place at which some Unionists expressed disapproval of O'Neill's actions. Sheelagh spoke in O'Neill's defence.

> I have heard nothing but widespread approval from the people to whom I have spoken for the Prime Minister's action. The whole country has [been], as it were, swept by a great wave of relief. It was as if the dead

1964 UK general election: South Down rally in Ardglass.
Major Hamilton Simmonds-Gooding (candidate), Albert McElroy,
Ted Taylor, Sheelagh Murnaghan and Stanley Archer

weight of history had been lifted from people's shoulders. The vast
majority of people feel they own him a great debt of gratitude.[20]

She mocked the hardline Unionist Edmund Warnock, whose speech
was 'rather like Rip Van Winkle emerging from his sleep.' O'Neill, she
said, had 'showed a sense of responsibility of a leader.'[21] She made a
plea that people would:

> put many things aside which have happened in the past and to get on
> with the job of making Northern Ireland and the whole of Ireland a
> better place to live and work in, a place of which any Irishman, North
> or South, can really be proud, and a place which is no longer to be
> looked on as the odd island on the western seaboard of Europe where
> nobody can be expected to behave in a rational manner.[22]

There were numerous other issues which she spoke on in Stormont
week in and week out – including nursery schooling, the 11+
selection exam process, fisheries, election reform, social welfare and
government compensation for rescue service volunteers injured in the
course of their job. Her standing in the Liberal Party was very high
and she was invited to speak at the UK Liberal Party assemblies. She
was in Brighton in 1963 when party leader Jo Grimond, who had

helped rebuild the party from a position of virtual extinction in the early 1950s, told the assembly that he was going to 'lead my troops towards the sound of gunfire.'[23] Back in Belfast, Sheelagh was elected as Honorary President of the newly founded Northern Ireland Federation of Young Liberals in November 1963.

In the 1964 UK general election the Liberals contested four of the twelve constituencies. Albert McElroy in North Down and Judith Rosenfield in South Belfast polled poorly but new ground was broken by Hamilton Simmonds-Gooding in South Down with 10 per cent and Giles FitzHerbert in Fermanagh and South Tyrone with 11 per cent (despite physical attacks during the campaign).

In January 1965 Sheelagh Murnaghan stood for election to Belfast City Council in a by-election but failed to win a seat.[24] Her election literature stated that:

> all our citizens, whatever their religion, have a vital part to play in Belfast's future. All must accept their share of responsibility for the common welfare and all must have equal opportunity of access to the benefits which community life has to offer. We must not allow our lives to be poisoned and our progress impeded by the events of the past.

In November 1965, Sheelagh defended her Stormont seat in a general election. This time she was in the rare position of being an unopposed Liberal candidate and she was comfortably returned. Her election campaign was a calm affair compared with Albert McElroy's experience in the Enniskillen constituency where his meetings were repeatedly broken up by violent Unionist mobs.[25] In the aftermath of the government decision to site the second university in Coleraine, Claude Wilton polled an impressive 7,418 votes (47 per cent) in the Londonderry City constituency against the sitting Unionist MP's 8,432 (53 per cent).

A few months later in March 1966, when a UK general election took place, the Liberals fielded three candidates in Northern Ireland. At just a fortnight's notice and with almost no election literature and few canvassers, Sheelagh stood in North Down. She was helped by Unionist MP George Currie who pointed out in his election address that 'this election had been forced on us, at great expense to the taxpayers, by the Liberal Party which had no hope of success and lost its deposit in North Down at the last election'.

Sheelagh secured 21.5 per cent of the poll – 10,582 votes. Her colleagues also did well, with John Quinn getting 9,586 votes in South Down, pushing the Republican into third place, and Richard Moore receiving 8,941 in North Antrim.[26] Sheelagh's supporters gleefully noted that she had received more votes in North Down than Jo Grimond got with a winning 9,605 in his Orkney and Shetland constituency.[27] This was the high point for Ulster Liberalism. In a by-election for a Queen's University seat in November 1966, Albert McElroy actually got a higher total than Sheelagh in the 1961 by-election, polling 2,968 votes, but he failed to be elected by 749 votes.[28]

Early in 1967, more Liberal branches were formed in places such as Ballymena, Portrush and Magee College.[29] In the local elections an active Young Liberal branch helped the party to gain a seat in Downpatrick. The party also spread across the Border, with Sheelagh among the speakers at an information meeting held in Dublin's Gresham Hotel on 24 February. Out of this meeting emerged the Liberal Party of Ireland, which was linked with the Ulster Liberals through a co-ordinating body called the Irish Liberal organisation which at Sheelagh's suggestion rotated the chairmanship between North and South annually.[30] Sheelagh addressed meetings of the Irish Liberals and of other organisations. In 1967 she led the British delegation at the Liberal International Conference in Oxford. The same year she 'demonstrated her internationalism' again when she was one of the Irish delegation at the International Hockey Conference in Cologne.

While Ulster Liberal Party members such as Albert McElroy and Giles FitzHerbert spoke in terms of the desirability of eventual Irish unification, Sheelagh took a different approach. In speeches such as the one given at Castleblayney in County Monaghan in February 1967, she said that 'Neither North nor South is ready for unity.' A united Ireland could only come about through consent and issues such as economics and healthcare and the power of the Catholic Church stood in the way of a united Ireland. While helping to build the Liberals in Northern Ireland and in the Republic, Sheelagh was by now concentrating her energies in parliament on the issues of human rights and equality. Between 1962 and 1969, she became an eloquent voice for the promotion of a Human Rights Bill, as well as seeking to have capital punishment completely abolished in Northern Ireland and defending the basic rights of Northern Ireland's Itinerant or Traveller community.

Notes

1 Maebh McNamara and Paschal Mooney, *Women in Parliament: Ireland 1918–2000* (Dublin, 2000), p. 229.
2 Constance Rynder, 'Sheelagh Murnaghan and the Ulster Liberal Party', *Journal of Liberal History*, no. 71 (Summer 2011), p. 16.
3 *Ulster Herald*, 2 Dec. 1961.
4 Northern Ireland House of Commons Reports [henceforth NIHC], vol. 50, col. 156–7 (7 Dec. 1961).
5 NIHC, vol. 50, cols 153–6 (7 Dec. 1961).
6 Ibid., col. 127.
7 Gordon Gillespie, 'The Ulster Liberal Party 1956–1973', MSSc thesis (Queen's University Belfast, 1984), p. 40.
8 Ibid., p. 14.
9 Ibid., p. 42.
10 NIHC, vol. 51, cols 231–5 (6 Mar. 1962).
11 Ibid., vol. 52, col. 1807 (4 Dec. 1962).
12 Ibid., vol. 53, col. 1672 (19 Mar. 1963).
13 Ibid., col. 1673.
14 Ibid., col. 1674.
15 Ibid., col. 1675.
16 Ibid., col. 1675.
17 Ibid., vol. 53, cols 148–9 (19 Mar. 1963).
18 Ibid., vol. 53, col. 283 (23 Jan. 1963).
19 Ibid., col. 233.
20 Ibid., vol. 59, col. 258, (3 Feb. 1965).
21 Ibid., col. 259.
22 Ibid., col. 257.
23 Berkley Farr, 'Liberalism in Unionist Northern Ireland', *Journal of Liberal Democrat History*, no. 33 (Winter 2001–02), p. 31.
24 Gillespie, 'The Ulster Liberal Party', p. 47.
25 Gordon Gillespie, *Albert McElroy: The Radical Minister 1915–1975* (Belfast, 1985), p. 22.
26 Gillespie, 'The Ulster Liberal Party', p. 48.
27 Berkley Farr, 'Liberalism in Unionist Northern Ireland', p. 31.
28 Gillespie, *Albert McElroy*, p. 25.
29 Gillespie, 'The Ulster Liberal Party', p. 55.
30 Ibid.

JOIN THE

ULSTER

LIBERAL

PARTY

Northern Ireland has no future unless the old hatred between Protestant and Catholic comes to an end. Bigotry, suspicion and mistrust must be removed from our community. The main aim of the Liberal Party is to end these divisions.

For too long the border issue has dominated Northern Ireland politics. Liberals were the first to state that the only sane attitude is to accept that there can be no change in Northern Ireland's basic constitutional position unless a majority of the people desire it.

What Northern Ireland needs is widespread support for a party composed of people from all creeds and classes dedicated to work together for the common good. This is what the Liberal Party is.

In this leaflet we outline a few of the things Liberals want to do and we ask for your support.

Election address and policy leaflet issued by Sheelagh Murnaghan for the 1969 general election for the Parliament of Northern Ireland (PRONI, D230/5/11/1)

5

Two Campaigns

Capital Punishment

The first human rights issue taken up by Sheelagh Murnaghan after her election was the abolition of the death penalty. In 1961 there were two executions in Northern Ireland. A month after Sheelagh's election Robert McGladdery was hanged in Belfast's Crumlin Road jail for the murder of Pearl Gamble in Newry. McGladdery was the last person to be executed in Northern Ireland.[1] Sheelagh's cousin Judge George Murnaghan had tried Michael Manning – the last man executed in the Republic of Ireland (in 1954).[2]

In February 1963, a motion calling for the abolition of capital punishment was tabled at Stormont by Nationalist Party leader Eddie McAteer. Sheelagh spoke in support of the motion, declaring:

> I want to see the abolition of capital punishment because I believe it to be wrong in the light of present day conditions. I am absolutely convinced by the abundance of evidence now available that the death penalty is not a deterrent to murder. There must be adequate punishment, reflecting society's condemnation of murder, but not the penalty of repeating the crime in a legalised and calculating manner.[3]

McAteer's motion was rejected by the government. In November 1963, Sheelagh brought forward her own 'Homicide and Criminal Responsibility' Bill. In this legislation, she sought the complete abolition of the death penalty, as well as addressing areas of the law on murder and manslaughter such as the defence of being 'guilty but insane', the defence of 'diminished responsibility', which had been introduced into English law in 1957 but not extended to Northern Ireland; and the law around 'culpable homicide.' One clause of the

Bill suggested substituting a fixed term of imprisonment – 65 years was her suggestion – as an alternative to the death penalty. She explained that she had done this because the public did not believe that 'life imprisonment' meant life and, in fact a 'life' sentence in Northern Ireland could mean as little as nine years. She argued that there was absolutely no evidence to support the belief that capital punishment was a deterrent.[4]

Sheelagh's Bill was seconded by the Northern Ireland Labour MP, Tom Boyd. He stated that:

> The Honourable and Learned lady has performed a service whether or not the Bill receives the full support of the house. The Bill and her supporting speech mark out the road which must be followed if the law in Northern Ireland is to be brought into line with modern thought.[5]

The government made it clear that they 'could not accept the Bill although 'there is much in the Bill that commends itself to them.' The areas of diminished responsibility and insanity would be examined but on the issue of capital punishment the government stood firm. The Bill was lost by 23 votes to 15.[6] However the government did indicate that it would bring in its own legislation on the matter.

In 1965, capital punishment was abolished in Great Britain and the Northern Ireland government brought in a Criminal Justice Bill in March 1966, which abolished the death penalty for most categories of murder but which retained it for the murder of police officers or prison warders or for murders carried out by the those pursuing 'subversive aims' – clearly a reference to the IRA.[7] During the debate on the Bill, Sheelagh argued that the death penalty would not protect police officers. 'I want to protect our police in abolishing the death penalty, we are giving the police a greater protection that they have at the moment.' Many policemen had been murdered over the years and 'their protection was no greater by the reason of the existence of the death penalty than it would have been without it.'[8] She also expressed concerns that giving the police special protections and setting them aside from ordinary citizens 'might reinforce the belief that the police were tools of the government rather than an independent force.' This angered some Unionist MPs, but she emphasised that she supported the police, regarded them highly and did not consider them to be anything other than impartial.[9] She was concerned that there were those in society who might seek martyrdom by killing a police officer or some other subversive act. She was aware – 'And I in no way wish to be associated with that view' – that there were those who saw police as 'legitimate subjects of attack' and who would regard the killing of a police officer as good propaganda for their cause.[10]

In a remarkable statement, Sheelagh set out the depth of her opposition to the death penalty:

> Supposing which, God forbid, that anybody should have it in his head to bump me off, I don't wish that the person or persons to suffer the death penalty for the reason that I no longer walk the earth. It would be no consolation to me in my last agony to know that my killer would hang by the neck.[11]

Despite Sheelagh's powerful words, the government insisted that 'capital punishment should be retained for the categories of murder of a police officer or prison warders and for murder done in the cause or furtherance of any seditious conspiracy.' The vote in favour of retention was 23 to 15.[12] Sheelagh was a member of the National Society for the Abolition of Capital Punishment and she continued to support abolition. The death penalty would finally be removed from the statute book in Northern Ireland by the UK government in July 1973.[13]

Travellers/Itinerants

An issue which Sheelagh raised time and time again during her career was the wellbeing and the basic human rights of the Traveller community in Northern Ireland. The Travellers – or Itinerants as they were then known – lived for the most part in deplorable conditions, camping on waste ground from which they were continually moved by local authorities, deprived of sanitation, running water or heating facilities. Most Traveller children were infrequent or non-school attenders, literacy rates were low, unemployment levels high and life expectancy considerably below the national average. Travellers were generally regarded with hostility and contempt by most settled people, Catholic and Protestant alike, and were seen as a problem for which there was no solution. There was absolutely no political advantage to being pro-Traveller, but in Sheelagh Murnaghan, Northern Ireland's most marginalised community found an outspoken defender. Year

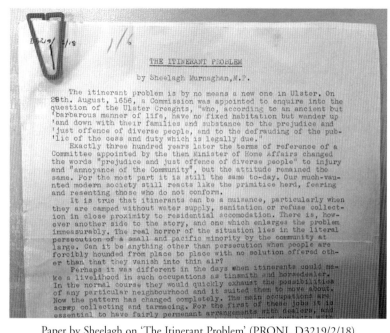

THE ITINERANT PROBLEM

by Sheelagh Murnaghan,M.P.

The itinerant problem is by no means a new one in Ulster. On 28th. August, 1656, a Commission was appointed to enquire into the question of the Ulster Creaghts, "who, according to an ancient but 'barbarous manner of life, have no fixed habitation but wander up 'and down with their families and substance to the prejudice and 'just offence of diverse people, and to the defrauding of the pub-'lic of the cess and duty which is legally due."

Exactly three hundred years later the terms of reference of a Committee appointed by the then Minister of Home Affairs changed the words "prejudice and just offence of diverse people" to injury and "annoyance of the Community", but the attitude remained the same. For the most part it is still the same to-day. Our much-vaunted modern society still reacts like the primitive herd, fearing and resenting those who do not conform.

It is true that itinerants can be a nuisance, particularly when they are camped without water supply, sanitation or refuse collection in close proximity to residential accomodation. There is, however another side to the story, and one which enlarges the problem immeasurably. The real horror of the situation lies in the literal persecution of a small and pacific minority by the community at large. Can it be anything other than persecution when people are forcibly hounded from place to place with no solution offered other than that they vanish into thin air?

Perhaps it was different in the days when itinerants could make a livelihood in such occupations as tinsmith and horsedealer. In the normal course they would quickly exhaust the possibilities of any particular neighbourhood and it suited them to move about. Now the pattern has changed completely. The main occupations are scrap collecting and tarmacing. For the first of these jobs it is essential to have fairly permanent arrangements with dealers, and

Paper by Sheelagh on 'The Itinerant Problem' (PRONI, D3219/2/18)

after year, she raised the issues of Traveller health, accommodation, schooling and welfare entitlements with government ministers, whose inclination was to do as little as possible.[14]

In 1968, for example, she spoke in a debate on providing houses or serviced halting sites for Traveller families. She suggested the necessity for three or four such halting sites around the country. Travellers would have to officially register to live on such sites, but they should 'still be allowed the freedom to live their own way of life and to move around from one site to another. These are things which cannot be enforced until provision is made by which they can be recognised as people and not be forced to live like animals.'[15]

A year earlier, during a debate on Traveller housing, Sheelagh had said: 'These people are not going to vanish into thin air. Thank goodness we have a democracy in existence, so that nobody is able at a whim to decide that a particular section of the community is invisible and to shift them over the border, as has been done in communist States.'[16] At a time when the Nazi genocide campaign against European Gypsies (or Roma) was hardly known and not officially acknowledged, Sheelagh reminded parliament (in which many veterans of the war against fascism sat) that 'The arch enemy of the itinerants, the gypsies of Europe was one Adolph Hitler.'

Sheelagh questioned the Minister for Health about national insurance and other benefits for Travellers. She questioned the Minister for Education about the inability of Traveller parents to send their children to school because of harassment by local authorities, who sometimes had their caravans moved up to three times a week. A question to the government in 1965 asked:

> What steps the Minister for Development was taking to provide sites for itinerants evicted by local authorities from sites they customarily occupy? I just want to ask the Minister whether the government are prepared to accept responsibility for a particular category of society which is part of our system whether or not he approves of it.[17]

She continued by drawing a parallel with the treatment of African Americans in the southern USA.

> Might I ask the Right Honourable gentleman to realise that we are not living down in Dallas, and that these unfortunate people are members of the human family for whom we have responsibilities? Does he not believe that the local authorities have a moral obligation not only to provide for these people's temporary well being but to look after their future well being? Is not that obligation being terribly violated day by day by the refusal to give them the facilities which are represented in this question?[18]

Sheelagh 'made little headway in her representations as the government regularly refused her requests.'[19] But she did not wait for the government to take action. In 1967, she helped found a school for Traveller children, St Paul's in Belfast. She worked with a cross-community group called the Assisi Fellowship, who helped look after the Traveller community in practical ways. She chaired the Belfast Itinerant Settlement Committee when it was formed in 1969.[20] She was a frequent visitor to Traveller caravans, where she was warmly welcomed. She tried to get work for Traveller men in areas such as scrap metal dealing. On one occasion she even took in a tramp – Jimmy – to lodge in her house. He stayed in the attic for some time.

Occasionally her generosity was taken advantage of by rogues, but she remained solid in her principles and in her opposition to prejudice and discrimination wherever it occurred. As she had stated in one of her election addresses: 'The application of basic Christian principles to the political life of Northern Ireland is the basis of my attitude to politics.'[21]

For Sheelagh Murnaghan, the equality of all people in Northern Ireland – regardless of colour, creed or social class, was a political belief and a principle for which she would fight throughout her career.

Notes

1   https://en.wikipedia.org/wiki/Capital_punishment_in_the_
     United_Kingdom, accessed 14 May 2019.
2   https://en.wikipedia.org/wiki/Michael_Manning_(murderer),
     accessed 14 May 2019.
3   Northern Ireland House of Commons Reports, vol. 52, col. 548
     (19 Mar. 1962).
4   NIHC, vol. 55, cols 1004–07 (19 Nov. 1963).
5   Ibid., cols 967–8.
6   Ibid., col. 1012.
7   Ibid., vol. 62, col. 1775, (3 Mar. 1966).
8   Ibid., cols 1775–6.
9   Ibid., col. 1777.
10 Ibid.
11 Ibid.
12 Ibid.
13 https://en.wikipedia.org/wiki/Capital_punishment_in_the_
     United_Kingdom, accessed 14 May 2019.
14 Paul Hainsworth (ed.), *Divided Society: Ethnic Minorities and
     Racism in Northern Ireland*, (London, 1998), pp 26–7.
15 NIHC, vol. 68, col. 1015.
16 Ibid.
17 Ibid., vol. 67, col. 1296.
18 Ibid., col. 1015.
19 Ibid., col. 1016.
20 Constance Rynder, 'Sheelagh Murnaghan and the Ulster Liberal
     Party', *Journal of Liberal History*, no. 71(Summer 2011), p. 18.
21 Interview with Fr Alec Reid, by Nick McGinley (nephew of
     Sheelagh Murnaghan), DVD (2004).

6

The Human Rights Bills

ON 16 JUNE 1964, SHEELAGH MURNAGHAN introduced her Human Rights Bill in parliament. This was the first human rights bill ever presented in a United Kingdom legislature.[1] The Bill was intended to uphold universal standards of human rights in Northern Ireland and to challenge and end the widespread practices of unfair discrimination in areas such as housing, employment and local government elections which, by the sixties, were causing increasing resentment among Catholics and which would cause the *Sunday Times* in 1966 to brand the Province as 'John Bull's Political Slum.'[2]

Since the foundation of Northern Ireland in 1922, only one political party, the Ulster Unionists, had held power. In order to retain power and prevent the Unionist vote from fragmenting, the government abolished Proportional Representation (PR) for local government in 1922 (ending George Murnaghan's ten-year tenure as Vice Chairman of Tyrone County Council) and for Stormont elections (except for Queen's University) in 1929.

Local government wards were gerrymandered in such a way that in Nationalist majority areas such as Londonderry (more often shortened to Derry, especially by Catholics), Omagh and Dungannon, Unionist voters elected more councillors than Nationalist voters. (In Derry, for example, this resulted in 12 Unionist and eight Nationalists being elected).[3] Property qualifications for voting which had been abolished in Great Britain were retained in Northern Ireland. Only ratepayers were entitled to vote. A person paying rates for business premises as well as his house had two votes. If he had two or three more business premises he would have two or three extra votes. Protestants as well as Catholics suffered from this denial of democracy. Housing allocation was in the hands of local councils and was used to give tenancies unfairly to political supporters and others regarded as 'our own people.' This resulted in long housing waiting lists in places such as Derry, Tyrone and Fermanagh, with big Catholic families often living in two- or three-room houses for years, while smaller Protestant families were given preference. In Derry, more than 200 families were packed into 160 Nissan huts on a former American military base called Springtown.

In 1959 a Derry City Councillor, Seamus Deeney, asked how 'a young married couple with one child could be given a higher degree of priority than a family of eight living in Springtown camp for the last eleven years? These people have a damned good case for the Human Rights Commission in Strasbourg.'[4]

In June 1964, when there were still over 150 families on the site, Sheelagh Murnaghan visited Springtown. Having praised the women of the camp for the way in which they carried on their daily chores in the face of such adversity', she stated: 'I have never seen anything as bad as this except in Johannesburg.'[5]

Employment was another area of inequality, with Catholics under-represented in many areas – including the big engineering and shipbuilding sectors. In the Northern Ireland civil service there were grades above which Catholics found it almost impossible to rise. Even at Queen's University employment among academic staff remained overwhelmingly Protestant even as the 1947 Education Act brought increasing numbers of working class grammar-school educated Catholics into tertiary education. This then was the situation in Northern Ireland when Sheelagh introduced her first bill.

In March of 1964, Sheelagh gave an indication of her concerns about discrimination and how prejudice and discrimination could be challenged when she spoke in debates on two bills before parliament. Taking part in a debate on Eddie McAteer's 'Diminution of Discord' Bill, she said:

> We won't get a better spirit in the community unless the government are prepared to remedy grievances where they do exist. It is the responsibility of the government to take any action which is necessary to remedy actual grievances. We have, in fact, a sick community, to say there is no practical action which can be taken is rather like saying

to someone who is ill, with TB, that there is no use treating that person for the disease – that everything will be all right when he gets better housing conditions.[6]

She spoke about the issue of housing and suggested that a points system should be put in place and that houses should be allocated on the basis of need and nothing else. The allocation of houses, she felt, should be taken out of the hands of local councillors. Analysing the nature of discrimination in the province she said:

> It is my firm conviction that the practise of discrimination, to the extent to which it exists, is essentially a political matter. It is really based on political considerations undoubtedly its impact is religious because of the unfortunate circumstance that because of one's religion, one's politics are assumed to follow on automatically.[7]

She concluded her speech by urging the government to take action to 'show not only the people of this country but the people of the world that a new day has dawned in Northern Ireland.'[8]

During a debate on a Racial Discrimination Bill for Northern Ireland in March 1964, Sheelagh welcomed the proposed legislation but complained that the Bill did not meet the specific needs of Northern Ireland where there were – as yet – few people of colour.

> I would state without fear of real contradiction that there are people in this country who are suffering from disadvantage to put it no higher. I think it is practically useless to employ the term discrimination which, although it may be technically accurate, is unfortunate. What I would rather do is to tackle the problem from the point of view of those who are actually suffering disadvantage rather than to try to tackle it from the point of view of trying to score off the other side. This is what we suffer from so badly in Northern Ireland. There are so few people who actually want to remedy the problems that exist. The emphasis all the time is on trying to put the blame on someone else. It may be immaterial who is greatest to blame for discrimination in Northern Ireland, but it is not the crux of the matter. The crux of the matter is to remedy the position of those who in fact do suffer disadvantage and who find themselves at a practical disadvantage in the community. I repeat that this is a factual problem. It is one which exists and no number of resolutions discussed at

young Unionist conferences will change the actual facts of the
situation. This is essentially a Human Rights problem.[9]

Sheelagh's first Human Rights Bill was intended to make certain
types of discrimination illegal and to provide a system to investigate
complaints. The Bill was modelled on two important overseas pieces
of Human Rights legislation. One was the Ontario Human Rights Act
in Canada which had come into existence in 1962 and which
outlawed discrimination on grounds of colour, creed, social class,
nationality and gender.[10] The other was the Equal Rights Act, which
was about to be signed into law in the United States. Article VII of
this Act also outlawed discrimination on grounds of colour, creed,
nationality or social class.[11]

In drawing up this Bill – Sheelagh took advice – as she would
continue to do from her cousin Frank D. Murnaghan, the son of the
mathematician. Frank D. Murnaghan, born in 1920, was a lawyer and
civil rights activist in law practice in Baltimore with a strong interest
in human rights and equality issues.[12] Introducing the Bill, Sheelagh
acknowledged that the law would not cure all Northern Ireland's
problems or change the minds of the prejudiced.

> One can't legislate unjust discrimination out of existence, one
> can, however, give a lead by which it's perfectly clear to every
> citizen what he may or may not do. One of the most terrible
> indictments of our community is that so many people here
> seem to regard religious discrimination as something which is
> normal and inevitable until the law can tell them in clear terms
> that they are wrong.[13]

The Bill prohibited discrimination in employment, housing and public
facilities, 'On the basis of race, creed, colour or political belief.' Trade
Unions were also prohibited from discrimination under the terms of
the Bill. The publication of statements promoting racial, sectarian or
political hatred was also prohibited; the punishment for those guilty of
discrimination was a £100 fine 'while any person suffering loss or
damage by reason of discrimination could recover damages by Civil
action.'[14] The Bill proposed the setting up of a Human Rights
Commission. The Commission would be made up of five members
appointed by the Northern Ireland government in consultation with

the Trade Unions and representatives of the main religious denominations. The chairman and his/her deputy would be appointed by the Queen's representative in Northern Ireland – the Governor. Funding for the commission would come from the Northern Ireland parliament and there would be a permanent secretariat.

The Commission would have the duty of inquiring into any cases complaining of discrimination brought before it and would be empowered to summon witnesses and to request the production of documents. Commission hearings would be held in private and the Commission would be able to make relevant recommendations to the government or public bodies. Sheelagh believed that it was vital that those who believed they were victims of discrimination had a body to which they could appeal and have their grievances heard. It was also vital that such a body should have real powers to act and that laws be enforced. The proposed Human Rights Commission was a first for the United Kingdom, only France and Ontario had such a commission at the time.[15]

The Bill was supported by the Northern Ireland Labour Party. During the course of his speech, the party leader, Tom Boyd, raised the issue of political discrimination by citing a case in Omagh in which a Labour Party supporter had allegedly been denied a house because of his politics. Boyd accused Nationalist councillors in Omagh of practising discrimination against socialists and noted that few Nationalist MPs had turned up for the debate. When the Bill went to a vote it was defeated by 23 votes to 17, Unionist MPs abstained or voted against. The government case against the Bill was that: (a) there was really no discrimination in Northern Ireland, so there was no need for the Bill; (b) if there was discrimination, Catholics were just as guilty as Protestants; and (c) legislation could not make people change their opinions or eliminate prejudice, so the Bill would not make a difference. Education was the answer to dealing with discrimination, not legislation.[16]

Sheelagh brought forward a second Human Rights Bill at the end of 1965, and this was debated on 8 February 1966. By now the political situation was changing. The Campaign for Social Justice (CSJ) had been set up in Dungannon by Patricia and Conn McCluskey to highlight the problems in housing and employment in Dungannon and elsewhere due to discrimination. The CSJ made it clear that they were not interested in partition or a united Ireland. They sought help from the Northern Irish and British authorities to deal with the problems faced in Dungannon and elsewhere and sought equality and all the benefits of British citizenship.[17] The CSJ distributed pamphlets, talked to the media in Britain and the Republic and went to meet British politicians. The Ulster Liberals supported their campaign.

A new British government was elected in October 1964. Labour were back in government and many of their MPs were becoming aware of the problems in Northern Ireland. In June 1965, two Labour politicians, Fenner Brockway and Paul Rose, along with an ebullient Irish immigrant and Labour Party member, Paddy Byrne, set up the Campaign for Democracy in Ulster (CDU). The CDU held its first meeting on 2 June. The emphasis was on political reform within Northern Ireland – not partition. All people in Northern Ireland were entitled to the full benefits and rights of equal citizenship. Byrne told the press that the Unionists could put up a wall along the border if they wished – so long as all those within the wall continued to enjoy 'full British benefits,'[18]

CDU members were soon meeting Northern Irish politicians and civil rights activists. The Liberal Party leader, Jo Grimond, met a delegation from the Nationalist Party and expressed 'shock' at the evidence presented to him concerning the situation in Derry.[19] The National Council for Civil Liberties held a conference on Northern Ireland in March 1965 at which Sheelagh Murnaghan represented the Ulster Liberals. She told the conference that, at this stage, proposals from some Labour MPs for a royal commission into the situation in the province was unnecessary and that it would be better if the North sorted out its problems itself.[20]

At this stage too, Terence O'Neill was reaching out to the Republic and there was hope for change and reform. However, as 1965 continued, Sheelagh, like others, became increasingly disillusioned with the government. The decisions to establish a new city in the Protestant-majority area of North Armagh and call it Craigavon annoyed Nationalists. In a stormy debate on the new city, Minister William Craig accused those opposing the name of being 'extreme Nationalists', to which Sheelagh retorted: 'I am not an extreme Nationalist and I think that Craigavon is a bad choice.'[21]

The decision to site the New University of Ulster in Protestant-majority Coleraine, County Londonderry, rather than in Catholic-majority Derry city – where there was already a third level college – also angered Nationalists. In a debate on the university question Harry Diamond noted that there had been high hopes that change was coming to Northern Ireland which meant that, 'The old bitterness of the past could be banished and these politics of discrimination would end.' Sheelagh interjected: 'All that could happen but this government will not do it.'[22]

And so, Sheelagh brought forward her Human Rights Bill again – in the hope that the government would do something. Introducing the Bill she said:

> This Bill is not a mere academic exercise. It is not a mere affirmation of principles. It is an attempt to provide a remedy for a situation which actually exists and which has existed for a long time. Injustice is the real cancer in our community and it must be cut out. It manifests itself most clearly and painfully in the field of local authority housing allocations and employment. It is utterly incredible that in a predominately Christian community a man's religion should be weighed against him in the balance in his daily life. Let me state categorically that there are degrees of citizenship in this country. Full citizenship requires that equal rights and opportunities should not only be not denied but that the law should be able to protect those rights.[23]

The Bill also contained a section on equal pay and gender discrimination in the workplace. This reflected the British Liberal Party's views and her own deep belief in equality for all. Again she looked to America for examples of equality legislation – in this case the 1963 Equal Pay Act and Title VII of the Civil Rights Act of 1964.[24]

Sheelagh explained to MPs that she had 'entertained the possibility that the whole subject of equal rights for women was such a far reaching one that it would be better dealt with by separate legislation.' She had put in the equal pay cause because 'the principle is exactly the same. The principle is that every citizen should be entitled to equal rights under the law and that the law and administrative machinery should be there to protect those rights.'[25]

This questioning of gender discrimination and of a deeply patriarchal society went unnoticed at the time 'with Press coverage mentioning only the Equal Pay aspect.'[26] But Sheelagh would return to the gender issue later in 1966 when she spoke during a debate on discrimination in public office appointments. She deplored the practice of limiting Catholic appointments to Catholic majority districts, and of favouring Protestants for supervisory positions. Noting that Catholics felt that they had to work twice as hard in order to prove themselves, she added: 'It is much the same sort of thing many women members of the community feel in regard to appointments. That they have to prove themselves to be better, and considerably better, than their colleagues in order to secure positions of high office.'[27]

In her speech on the Human Rights Bill, Sheelagh acknowledged the work being done by the Campaign for Social Justice and also praised 'those who have spoken out from what I describe as the majority side of the house. People in all sections of the community are now acknowledging that the time has come to speak out against this evil thing in our midst.'[28] She took on the argument that the constitution and parliament of Northern Ireland did not discriminate:

> It is by conduct that the people of the minority religion in Northern Ireland have suffered a diminution of their rights. The effect for the individuals is almost the same as if he was discriminated against by an act of parliament. Conduct in the public sector and in the private sector combined to provide the situation in which almost every Roman Catholic is conscious of the possibility that at one time or another his religion is going to be held against him.[29]

When government MPs argued that the Constitution of Northern Ireland (the 1920 Government of Ireland Act) provided protection, she responded by saying that:

> Discrimination in practice stems from conduct rather than from an enactment of our parliament. The law as it stands provides absolutely no remedy for a person who is unjustly treated. The Government of Ireland Act says nothing whatever about discrimination in the private sector. The large field of private enterprise is completely untouched by our Constitution.[30]

The Bill was supported by the Northern Ireland Labour Party, Republican Labour and a few Nationalist MPs, but opposed by the majority of Unionists. When the argument was put up that there was no need for legislation, Sheelagh retorted angrily:

> It is not for those who do not know what it is like to be on the receiving end to say that there is no need for a remedy. In my opinion discrimination is not something which should be lamented and forgotten about. It is something to be angry about. While there is one case of discrimination people should be concerned.[31]

In response to government arguments that the discrimination legislation would not work and would only create tension, she responded:

> These are arguments which have been visited before. They have been used in this and other jurisdictions. Various States of the USA and the provinces of Canada which have implemented legislation of this kind have also had to contend with those who asserted that you cannot legislate against feelings, or that legislation would only harden attitudes. Experience has proved them wrong. The fact is that laws can lessen the impact of discrimination and in so doing they diminish the prejudice which is at the root of discrimination. Practical experience had shown that the curbing of discriminatory practices tends to bring about a lessening of prejudice and that when people are keen to combat an unhealthy social custom they are glad to have the support of the law behind them.[32]

She urged the government to take action, even if they would not accept the Bill – she suggested that they could 'act positively in some other way' by taking housing and local authority appointments out of the hands of local councils, and withhold grants or other support from private companies who 'refuse employment on the basis of religion or race.' If the government were not to take action 'to see that the majority have equal opportunities for advancement it is undoubtedly very difficult to escape the conclusion that the aim is to keep things that way.'[33]

As on other occasions Sheelagh addressed the issue of Northern Ireland's standing in the world.

It is no joy to me to wash Northern Ireland's dirty laundry in public but that is not a reason for denying the existence of the dirty linen – one of the factors which we must take into account and keep always in our mind is the good name of Northern Ireland. We are all citizens of this country. We are proud of this country. None of us enjoys a situation in which a finger can be pointed at us as an area where unhealthy discriminatory practices arise. It is a very sad indictment on a country which is supposed to be and I believe is profoundly Christian in its outlook. In the name of Christianity of Justice and of Northern Ireland, I commend this Bill to the House.[34]

The Bill was rejected by 26 votes to nine. Sheelagh indicated that if the government did not take action, she would seek help from London. She told MPs:

I have always taken the view that the problem of discrimination is one for the Northern Ireland parliament, but if I don't receive some intimation today that the government are prepared to act I shall have no option but to join forces with those who take the view that the remedy must be sought from the Westminster Parliament.[35]

By now the situation in Northern Ireland was beginning to deteriorate. The commemorations of the fiftieth anniversary of the 1916 Rising and the Battle of the Somme raised communal tensions. In July, loyalist extremists murdered three people – two Catholic men and a Protestant woman in a series of gun and petrol bomb attacks. In June Rev. Ian Paisley, as head of a rival church, led a crowd through Belfast to protest violently against ecumenism outside the Presbyterian General Assembly. Sheelagh condemned the protest:

I do not think anybody can be blamed for questioning whether some of the things that have been done recently in the name of religion have anything at all to do with religion as a Christian should know it. The type of methods which are used to stir up the fervour of the followers of this man [Paisley] are merely the dissemination of a poison in our community.

The Civil Rights Movement was growing. In August a meeting in Dungiven organised by the republican Wolfe Tone Society began to lay the groundwork for a Civil Rights Association. At Westminster,

THE HUMAN RIGHTS BILLS

Gerry Fitt, newly elected Republican Labour MP for Belfast West, was keeping the Campaign for Democracy in Ulster informed about the situation in Northern Ireland. He managed to challenge the convention that matters devolved to the Northern Ireland parliament be not raised at Westminster. Fitt had supported Sheelagh's Human Rights and Capital Punishment Bills and she liked him.[36]

Back at Stormont, Sheelagh tried to keep up the pressure on the government to accept the reality of discrimination and to take steps to end it. In November 1966, during a debate on appointments, she asked the Home Affairs Minister:

> Whether he is absolutely and utterly satisfied and can honestly answer this question, that it is never held against a Catholic applicant for a post or where a Catholic might expect to be appointed in circumstances where there is not the position of an actual application, being, put in, that he is a Roman Catholic. I am absolutely convinced, it is an incontrovertible fact that a Roman Catholic is at a disadvantage as against a Protestant of approximately equal or equivalent qualifications. This is what is at the centre of the problem – the absolute knowledge on the part of the Roman Catholic population that they have to go one better – to be way above the standard of the opposing Protestant applicant or applicants when they apply for a job.
>
> May I ask the Minister to face the fact that the denial of the existence of an advantageous position for Protestants over Roman Catholics is a factor in our system, and to ask him to lend his mind to getting rid of this thing in our community which produces the suspicion, lack of community feeling and lack of the necessary co-operation from the minority of which we are always accused. I ask him to recognise that a lack of opportunity to participate or to rise to posts of responsibility is as much a factor as any lack of willingness on the part of the minority in this population to play its full part in our country's activities.[37]

Unfortunately, the government showed little or no sign of listening to Sheelagh or to others who argued for reform before it was too late.

The area where reform was called for was the electoral system – the lack of PR and the lack of 'one man, one vote' at local government level. One of the Liberal Party's main policy positions across the

United Kingdom was the introduction of a PR system. In parliament, Sheelagh put the case for the Single Transferrable Vote (STV) – PR system to be restored to Northern Ireland in the interests of democracy 'so that all sections of the community get a fair representation and all votes are of equal value.'[38]

However, the only reform offered by the O'Neill administration was the abolition of the Queen's University seat. University seats in Great Britain had been abolished in 1948, so Sheelagh was not opposed to the abolition of her seat as such. What did anger her was that the government refused to abolish the multiple votes available to businessmen and some householders. She understood that the government was willing to abolish the Queen's constituency because they could not be certain of winning the four seats there, while the multiple business vote helped prop up the Unionist vote. 'The government will stand indicted as a government which is prepared to implement democratic principles except where it happens to be for the convenience of the ruling party.'[39]

In February 1967, for the third time, Sheelagh brought a Human Rights Bill before Stormont. The Bill came up for debate just a couple of days after a visit to Ireland by the new British Liberal Party Leader, Jeremy Thorpe. Thorpe, whose father was Irish by birth, had a great interest in human rights issues. At a press conference in Belfast, following meetings with local Liberals, Thorpe expressed his hope that Sheelagh's Bill would be passed. He made clear his deep distaste for the local government voting system describing it as 'ridiculous and abominable', and stated that, while the Liberal Party supported devolution for the nations of the United Kingdom, 'Stormont was not a good example of government devolution.' Thorpe praised Sheelagh and her colleagues, saying that 'The Liberal Party had a great contribution to make to Northern Ireland politics.' He believed that it was 'necessary' to have an anti-discrimination Bill in Northern Ireland.[40]

Sheelagh's third Bill was broadly similar to the previous ones, but she made a few changes, dropping the proposed £100 fine for those guilty of discrimination and putting more emphasis on conciliation processes. As before, she looked to the United States for guidance when drafting her Bill. The new advisor for the legislation was Professor Arthur Bonfield of the University of Iowa Law School.

Professor Bonfield was a Civil Rights activist who wrote extensively on anti-discrimination law and the ways in which society could combat prejudice. During the debate, Sheelagh quoted extensively from his articles and even brought copies of the *Iowa Law Journal* into parliament so that MPs might read Bonfield's work (few did so). She also quoted from a speech given by John F. Kennedy in 1963 in which the President, observing that the US Constitution declared that all men are created equal, 'stemming from this precept is the obligation to build social institutions that will guarantee equality of opportunity to all men regardless of their race, religion or national origin.' She introduced the Bill by stating that it was,

> An honest attempt to deal with a matter which has been the bane of Northern Ireland since the beginning of its existence. We have not managed over the years to shake off our reputation as a community plagued by prejudice and bias leading to unjust discrimination. I regret to say that this is a reputation which our community continues to earn.[41]

While welcoming the improvement in community relations which had taken place, she went on: 'The very fact that this improvement has evidenced itself is justification for a renewed demand that basic Human Rights should be enshrined in legislation.'[42] The basic concept of the Bill, she explained is the implementation of Human Rights.

> As yet we have no colour problem; but who can say that we will be without one for ever and a day? We certainly have a problem with regard to religious affiliation. There is no doubt whatever that the assumption that it is right and proper that members of one religious denomination or sectarian division should look after their own people, that this is, as it were, a law of nature, is an evil which pervades our whole political structure.[43]

She explained that the Bill was not intended to protect one particular group from discrimination. 'The Bill lays down that it is wrong to take religious affiliation into account with regard to basic Human Rights.' With regard to the argument put forward from the government side that laws could not change the way people thought, she quoted Bonfield's statement that 'changes in conduct required by Law, have in fact lessened prejudice.'

Sheelagh argued that the law was necessary because 'almost all of us from time to time require the backing of the law in order that we insist on taking what we know to be the right course.'[44] Laws against discrimination could, if enforced, reduce feelings of prejudice. To the argument that such laws could not be enforced, she again quoted Bonfield: 'The only requirement for enforcing legislation is the provision of satisfactory machinery for the purpose.' And, as she pointed out: 'many States of the USA and Canada, have in fact introduced legislation which has proved to be enforceable.'

What Sheelagh had in mind to investigate claims of discrimination was 'a body charged with responsibility for the enforcement and supervision of Human Rights. I have adopted the system of a Human Rights Commission.'[45]

The Commission would be made up of five people, with a full-time salaried chairperson to the Commission. Those who felt themselves to be victims of discrimination could take their case. At first it might be difficult to prove discrimination, but gradually 'a pattern would begin to emerge' when many cases could be examined. The Commission would have power to summon witnesses and to gather documents. Hearings would take place in private. Those approached by the Commission to answer accusations of discrimination might – through a policy of conciliation, change their ways. 'The man without a house might find himself on the housing list. The person refused admission to a club because of his religion might suddenly find his membership accepted.'[46]

Conciliation had worked in upwards of 80 per cent of cases in the USA. Those who did not obey the Commission's order to end discrimination would be guilty of contempt of court. The Bill also required the Commission 'to study the problem of discrimination in general, to issue periodic reports, to make recommendations to parliament and, generally review the situation. Other clauses in the Bill required Trade Unions to act towards all their members in the same way 'irrespective of race, colour, creed or political belief.' And, as in the previous Bill, Sheelagh tried to 'deal with the very ancient, vexed question of equal pay for equal work' as between male and female employees.[47]

Once more, Sheelagh reflected on how Northern Ireland was perceived in Britain and elsewhere. 'This problem of prejudice in our community is the main thing which brings our whole State and people into disrepute.' She feared that the prejudice rife in Northern Ireland was driving people away from religion because they could not stomach the way religion had been 'prostituted' in the name of tribal bigotry, and she worried too that too many people were now 'opting out' of their 'political responsibilities – unwilling to involve themselves in politics or government.[48]

The Bill was supported by Austin Carrie of the Nationalist Party and by the Republican and Northern Ireland Labour MPs. The debate was poorly attended. Terence O'Neill was now under pressure from the government in London to address the Civil Rights issue, but he was also under pressure from the right wing of his own party not to make concessions. And so the government refused to accept the Bill and it was defeated by 24 votes to seven. Sheelagh told the House: 'I hope and pray before I leave this House through the abolition of my seat in a few years' time that legislation against discrimination will have been enacted. If that should happen I feel that my time here will not have been completely wasted.'[49]

A few weeks after the rejection of Sheelagh's Bill, the Northern Ireland Civil Rights Association (NICRA) came into being, pledged to combat discrimination in housing, employment, voting rights and other areas, NICRA declared that partition was not the issue. What was required was to ensure that all the people of Northern Ireland enjoyed the full rights of British citizenship. NICRA had a thirteen member committee which included all sections of political opinion save the most extreme loyalists.[50] The Liberal Party was represented on the committee of NICRA by John Quinn from South Down. The chairperson was Betty Sinclair from Belfast who was a prominent trade unionist from a Protestant background and a member of the Communist Party. She and Sheelagh knew each other through common interest in Travellers Rights and Civil Rights and they got on well. Sheelagh welcomed the setting up of NICRA and was particularly pleased by the fact that the rights of Travellers were on the Association's agenda. The eviction of 45 Traveller families (400 people) from a halting site without any attempt to find them alternative accommodation led Sheelagh, having failed to get answers from a government Minister, to state that 'this society is so steeped in the acceptance of prejudice that the government do not see it even when it is under their noses.'[51]

Against the background of continuing government refusal to bring in reforms, Sheelagh planned to try once again to bring in a Human Rights Bill. The Campaign for Democracy in Ulster – which had supported Sheelagh's Bill, continued to send MPs over to see what life was like in Northern Ireland. What they saw shocked them. Paul Rose commented: 'On my visit to Dungannon I saw segregated housing estates which would have done credit to South Africa.' Maurice Miller – a Glasgow MP, who, like Paul Rose, was of Jewish, not Irish Catholic background, and so neutral in Northern Ireland's tribal division, stated 'with all its problems and difficulties there is more democratic right in India than in Northern Ireland.'[52]

The year 1967 marked the hundredth anniversary of the Fenian rising. The hardline Home Affairs Minister, William Craig, banned commemorative marches and outlawed the Republican Clubs on the grounds that they were an IRA front organisation. As the clubs were represented on the NICRA Committee, this ban caused particular resentment and Sheelagh voiced her anger to the Minister for what she regarded as an undemocratic action: 'The Minister in taking this step has been activated more by concern for the peace and good order of his own party than for the peace, order and good governance of Northern Ireland as a whole.'[53]

As part of her Human Rights campaign, Sheelagh wished to see an end to the Special Powers Act. First enacted in 1922 as a temporary measure against the IRA, the Act had been made permanent in 1932. The Act granted the Minister of Home Affairs authority to ban meetings, parades, publications and organisations whenever he deemed it necessary. The Special Powers Act was very rarely used against Loyalist parades or organisations – only against Nationalist groups. The Ulster Liberals and Civil Rights groups saw it as an Act used by the Unionists to curtail dissent. (Albert McElroy commented that trying to operate an opposition party in Northern Ireland was 'like running an underground movement in an occupied country.')

Sheelagh was particularly concerned about the powers given by the Act to the government to introduce internment or to authorise police raids without warrants into private homes. She regarded such powers as: 'A direct infringement on personal liberty that was unjustifiable in any circumstances.'

The year 1968 was designated by the United Nations as International Human Rights Year to mark the twentieth Anniversary of the Universal Declaration of Human Rights. To mark the occasion, Sheelagh brought her Human Rights Bill before Stormont once more. Addressing virtually empty government benches, she said: 'This is the fourth time since I came into this House that I have attempted to get the government to recognise the need for some form of Human Rights Legislation.'[54]

She quoted Article 8 of the Universal Declaration of Human Rights. 'Everyone has the right to an effective remedy by the competent National Tribunals for Acts violating the fundamental rights granted him by the Constitution or by Law.' She then quoted from Section 5 of the Government of Ireland Act: 'No preference, privilege or advantage shall be given to, nor shall any disability or disadvantage be imposed on any person on account of religious belief.' We have that principle enunciated in our Constitution', 'but the difficulty is that there is no effective remedy by the competent National Tribunals for Acts violating the fundamental rights granted by Section 5.'[55]

Her Bill sought to provide a remedy for anyone 'who has suffered a violation of his fundamental rights.' She then referred to comments made by the Attorney General during the debate on her 1967 Bill, to the effect that 'nobody could possible think it was an offence to prefer to employ someone of one's creed or colour' – a remark Sheelagh had found shocking. 'This is what Human Rights are about. This is what the Legislation enacted in various parts of the world has been mainly concerned with. It has been concerned with the problems of people preferring to house or to employ people of their own race or colour.'[56]

She then went on to read from a report into the workings of Britain's 1965 Race Relations Act and of anti-discrimination laws in the USA, which showed that such laws worked at reducing prejudice and that many that had opposed such laws had come to accept them and work them. Every progressive country, she went on,

Is finding it increasingly necessary to regulate this situation of infringement of basic rights and to enshrine in law even accepted rights. I wish I could feel I was talking to people who had made some sort of study on the subject. I hope the Minister will be able to tell me that somebody behind the scenes has been given the job of actually studying the subject because it is perfectly obvious to date, judging by previous debates, that no-one on the government side of the House has made a study of it. One has a ghastly feeling that one is talking to people who literally have not a clue.[57]

She continued by saying that she believed her Bill was necessary. It was necessary 'To enshrine in Law basic Human Rights and above all to give people an opportunity to have any violation of their rights investigated and, if necessary put right.'

She dismissed any comparison between Northern Ireland and places such as South Africa 'where fundamental Human Rights are treated with complete contempt.' 'But we have a specific problem here and I have no doubt the Commission would find enough work to justify its existence.'[58]

The Human Rights Commission she proposed would have the function of investigating complaints and to decide whether there have been violations of rights. She suggested that the Commission Chairman could also function as an Ombudsman. Complaints could be made by either individuals or the Commission itself. This part of the Bill 'drew on the workings of Commissions in the USA and Canada'. There was emphasis on having a procedure of conciliation, 'which experience elsewhere has shown normally leads to a satisfactory outcome.' If conciliation failed, then there would be a public inquiry held before the Commission to be chaired by a Judge – a procedure similar to that used in Ontario, Canada. There would be a right of appeal by either a complainant or a respondent to the Court of Appeal.

Clause 14 of the Bill 'Prohibits unlawful discrimination on the basis of race, creed, colour or political view in relation to employment.' In Clause 15 Sheelagh turned again to the question of equal pay for equal work. The Clause emphasised:

> The right of female employees to equal pay and for promotion and advancement. This is something which has been the cause of complaint for as long as women have been employed outside the home. In industry particularly this is very apparent.

Noting that women employed in manual work were being paid slightly above that paid to equivalent male workers, Sheelagh said:

This is something which cannot possibly be justified. The disparity is something that cannot be countenanced in a just society. I cannot conceive of any just argument in the case of a job, which is clearly the same job with exactly the same conditions and everything else, for paying someone less merely by reason of the accident of sex. This will have to be faced in due course.[59]

Clause 18 of the Bill dealt with housing:

No-one need try to tell me that housing is not one of the areas for discrimination in Northern Ireland. We all know that it is particularly taken for granted that in certain areas people will only get houses if they are of a certain religion. It occurs sufficiently often to be a real source of discord in the community. This is one of the outstanding fields where there has to be a very strong directive from the government and this House, that this practice of allocating Local Authority Housing on the basis of religion has to stop. It is something which must be made absolutely clear. I can think of no way to make it clearer than of enshrining it in law and making it a subject which can be investigated and any violation remedied.[60]

The Bill also looked at the area of private tenancies and house sales.

What justification can there possibly be for saying that a person selling his house is entitled to say: 'I refuse to sell this house to a Negro, a Catholic or a Jew.' The acceptance of this is a normal thing even for the Attorney-General. That is what I am trying to fight in this House. This is the main difficulty, that of trying to get through the mental block on the other side of the House. They just do not see anything wrong with such an attitude.[61]

The Bill also sought to prohibit discrimination by shops, pubs, hotels, garages and lodging houses. With regard to the lodgings, Sheelagh took note of the increasingly international student body at Queen's University and among her own constituents.

People should not be able to refuse to take in coloured students. In practise one generally finds the assumption that it would be quite impossible for a Catholic to take a Protestant into his house or vice versa, or a coloured person, when those who have had the courage to, as it were, experiment have by and large come to the conclusion that their original fears were pure myth.

Sheelagh went on to explain that:

> One of the aims of this type of legislation is to break down prejudice and therefore in no way should any of its provisions encourage the perpetuation of any of the prejudices which exist. That would be my basic approach to the matter. The whole point of this legislation is to back up people who do not want to discriminate. One must give every possible encouragement and assistance to those who wish to eliminate this type of practise from our community.

She then turned to the role of government. She pointed out that, in the USA, 'one of the most effective instruments against discrimination has been the government policy of inserting a clause in all public contracts which would provide for penalties if any discrimination is exercised by the contractor or any sub-contractor.' Sensing that her Bill would be once more rejected, she begged the government to put in such a clause themselves. 'This would go a very long way to changing the climate of opinion and particularly to breaking the attitude to which I have already referred, that choosing people of one's own sort is a perfectly proper and right thing to do.'[62]

She also touched on issues such as the possible need for affirmative action politics to help certain communities such as Travellers (Itinerants). 'I have already referred to the problem of Itinerants in our community, if that is not a Human Rights problem, I do not know what is.'[63]

She stated that in Human Rights year:

> The whole question of how one implements the United Nations Declaration should be considered. We should at least, if nothing else, be prepared to see that the provisions of our own constitution, that is Government of Ireland Act, Section 86, can be put into effect and that the citizens may be in a position to avail themselves of the rights granted in that part of the Constitution.

She dealt with the government claim that the constitution of Northern Ireland prohibited discrimination, so legislation was not needed. 'The whole point is that rights, unless they are enshrined in the law, are not rights at all.'[64]

> What I have asked for is an effective remedy, which is what the Bill is designed to promote. It is no answer for the Minister to repeat that there is a remedy under the existing law because in practise there is no such thing. What I have being trying to ask this House to do is to enshrine in the law certain basic rights which I think most people will acknowledge every individual should have. It is not much consolation to the man with a young family who is frantically trying to get a house to live in and who sees someone with much less need put into a Local Authority house to be told: 'Never mind old chap, things will be getting better and this sort of thing will probably not happen in ten years' time.' What that man wants is a remedy for the injustice which he sees.

The human rights commission could be 'an umbrella, a protection, somebody to whom the citizen can go.'[65] Once more the opponents of the Bill claimed that legislation would not be enforceable. Sheelagh replied to this by saying:

> I spend most of my opening speech trying to tell the House about how that sort of thing has been legislated for in other jurisdictions. We cannot legislate for people's minds. We cannot legislate to make them change their minds, but we can legislate about the way people put their opinions into practise. The very existence of legislation can have an effect of gradually getting people to alter their opinions.[66]

The government benches remained largely empty throughout the debate. Feeling that the Bill was facing defeat, Sheelagh said: 'I fear that once again we are going to be met with no consideration of the actual detailed terms and an out and out rejection.' The Bill was supported by Harry Diamond, who praised Sheelagh for 'her persistence,' and by Austin Currie. But when it came to a vote, the Bill was defeated by 22 votes to eight. Even moderate Unionists such as Bessie Maconachie, a fellow Queen's University MP, voted against it – despite acknowledging the 'existence of discrimination.' Those who turned up to reject the Bill included the Prime Minister, Terence O'Neill, and his two successors as Prime Minister, James Chichester-

Clark and Brian Faulkner. Harry Diamond angrily called it a 'vote for bigotry.' Sheelagh told the House:

> Legislation like this will be passed some time for this jurisdiction. The sooner it is done the more value it will have. It may not be in my time in the House but it will come some time. There will have to be acknowledgement of the necessity to regularise this area of Human Rights. I wish that the government had had the wit to face this thing now. One welcomes any move towards improvement of community relations but I think that this is the sort of thing which would provide a significant turning point and one which would be a real earnest of the government's serious intention to end the scourge of prejudice.[67]

It would 'be more than thirty years before a Northern Ireland legislative body addressed this issue again in such depth.'[68] Despite her failure to get her Human Rights Bills passed, Sheelagh had 'planted a seed.' Much of the reform legislation she spent her parliamentary career trying to achieve would eventually be passed. But the refusal of the Northern Ireland government to accept her Bills would have terrible consequences. The campaign for civil rights and reform was about to move from parliament to the streets.

Notes

1   Brice Dickson, *The European Convention on Human Rights and Conflict in Northern Ireland* (Oxford, 2012), p. 14.

2   Jonathan Bardon, *A History of Ulster*, (Belfast, 1992), p. 647.

3   Ibid.

4   http://www.nicivilrights.org/articles/springtown-camp-and-civil-rights-women/, accessed 14 May 2019.

5   http://springtowncamp.com/, accessed 14 May 2019.

6   Northern Ireland House of Commons Reports, vol. 56, col. 1422–3 (2 Mar. 1964).

7   Ibid., col. 1665–6 (10 Mar. 1964).

8   Ibid., vol. 56, col. 1424 (10 Mar. 1964).

9   Ibid., col. 1421 (2 Mar. 1964).

10 https://en.wikipedia.org/wiki/Ontario_Human_Rights_Commission, accessed 14 May 2019.

11 https://en.wikipedia.org/wiki/Civil_Rights_Act_of_1964#Title_ VII%E2%80%94equal_employment_opportunity, accessed 14 May 2019.
12 Constance Rynder, 'Sheelagh Murnaghan and the Struggle for Human Rights', *Irish Studies Review*, vol. 14, no. 4 (2006), pp 454, 458, n. 5.
13 NIHC, vol. 57, col. 1990 (16 June 1964).
14 Ibid., col. 1990.
15 Brice Dickson, *The European Convention on Human Rights*, p. 14.
16 NIHC, vol. 57, col. 95.
17 https://cain.ulster.ac.uk/events/crights/pdfs/csj179.pdf, accessed 14 May 2019.
18 https://cain.ulster.ac.uk/events/crights/purdie/purdie90_chap3.pdf (p. 108), accessed 14 May 2019.
19 Ibid., chapter 2, p. 77.
20 Conn McCluskey, *Up off their Knees: A Commentary on the Civil Rights Movement in Northern Ireland* (Dublin, 1989), p. 25.
21 NIHC, vol. 61, col. 2338 (20 Oct. 1965).
22 Ibid., col. 2339.
23 Ibid., vol. 62, col. 686 (8 Feb. 1966).
24 Ibid., vol. 62, col. 685.
25 Ibid., vol. 62, col. 691, (8 Feb. 1966).
26 Rynder, 'Sheelagh Murnaghan and the Struggle for Human Rights', p. 449.
27 NIHC, vol. 64, col. 2461 (17 Nov. 1966).
28 Ibid., vol. 62, col. 685 (8 Feb. 1966).
29 Ibid., vol. 64, col. 686.
30 Ibid., col. 688.
31 Ibid., col. 744.
32 Ibid., col. 687.
33 Ibid., col. 688.
34 Ibid., col. 693.
35 Ibid., col. 693.
36 Interview with Lucille McGinley, 2 Aug. 2017.
37 NIHC, vol. 64, col. 2450 (17 Nov. 1966).
38 Ibid., vol. 64, cols 339–40.
39 Ibid., vol. 62, col. 2019 (15 Apr. 1966).
40 *Irish Press*, 5 Feb. 1967.
41 NIHC, vol. 65, col. 925 (7 Feb. 1967).
42 Ibid., col. 927.

43 Ibid., col. 930.
44 Ibid., col. 932.
45 Ibid., col. 935.
46 Ibid.
47 Ibid.
48 Ibid., cols 937–9.
49 Ibid., col. 939.
50 Bardon, *History of Ulster*, p. 642.
51 NIHC, vol. 68, col. 669.
52 *Irish Press*, April 17 1967.
53 NIHC, vol. 66, col. 184 (16 Mar. 1967).
54 Ibid., vol. 68, cols 573–4 (30 Jan. 1968).
55 Ibid., col. 576.
56 Ibid., col. 577.
57 Ibid., col. 578
58 Ibid., col. 578.
59 Ibid., col. 582.
60 Ibid., col. 584.
61 Ibid., col. 584.
62 Ibid., col. 585.
63 Ibid., col. 585.
64 Ibid., col. 586.
65 Ibid., col. 586.
66 Ibid., col. 587.
67 Ibid., col. 608.
68 Constance Rynder, 'Sheelagh Murnaghan and the Ulster Liberal
      Party', *Journal of Liberal History*, no. 71 (Summer 2011), p. 17.

7

The Voice of Reason

SHEELAGH'S HUMAN RIGHTS BILL was defeated on 31 January 1968. A few weeks later there was a by-election for the Stormont constituency of Lisnaskea and the Liberals fielded a candidate, Stanley Wynne – hoping to benefit from a split Unionist vote and to gain Nationalist support. During the campaign, Lady Brookeborough, the mother of the Ulster Unionist candidate, attacked the Liberals, stating that they were no good. 'There is one Liberal in parliament, already and she never votes with the government.'[1] In the election, the Liberals came in third, failing to attract much Catholic support. Although the party was still apparently in good strength, with Young Liberal branches right across the country (including one in Omagh), the party was beginning to lose ground as Northern Ireland's tribal divisions re-emerged.[2]

The Liberals were themselves divided on the constitutional issue. Some were unionists who supported the union with Great Britain. Others were nationalists who supported the idea of a united Ireland with the consent of the majority of the people of Northern Ireland. Views also differed on how to bring about reforms. Some Liberals believed that street protests were now the only way to get reform while others, like Albert McElroy, dreaded the consequences of bringing protestors onto the streets.[3]

In June 1968, Austin Currie, who had supported Sheelagh's Human Rights Bills, took part in a Northern Ireland Civil Rights Association (NICRA) protest – a so called 'sit-in' in a house in Caledon against the allocation of the house to a single Protestant woman when a large Catholic family on the housing list needed it. A few weeks later, NICRA held its first public march in Dungannon.[4] On 5 October 1968, a civil rights march in Derry ended in violence. Television footage of the police officers batoning marchers, including Gerry Fitt, was seen around the world.

This was the turning point. As civil rights marches began to attract thousands of people and loyalist counter-demonstration brought out thousands more, the British government put O'Neill under pressure to start granting the demands of the Civil Rights marches. On 9 October, Sheelagh herself took part in a protest march by Queen's students. Blocked from reaching City Hall by Loyalist counter-protestors and the police, the students staged a sit down in Linenhall Street. Sheelagh, along with Betty Sinclair, urged common sense as the students debated whether to confront the police. Eventually they dispersed peacefully.[5]

In a debate in Stormont in the aftermath of the events in Derry, Sheelagh was critical of government and of the police and fearful of what the Derry events could lead to:

> The situation which has arisen is far too serious for this House to be indulging in debates about who said what. We must face the fact that the country is involved in a turmoil which requires the utmost level-headedness from all sections of the community and particularly from government spokesmen.[6]

Calling for an inquiry to be set up into the Derry debacle, she recalled how the Minister for Home Affairs, William Craig, had refused to answer her questions about what orders had been given to the police that day. The Prime Minister had stated that an inquiry would undermine police confidence. To this Sheelagh responded: 'Nothing would be more calculated to undermine the confidence of the police than the feeling that they are going to have to accept the blame for anything that goes wrong in the carrying out of government orders.'[7]

She laid the blame for the lack of confidence in the police and the polarisation of the country on the government's actions: 'Actions which to the people have seemed so blind and unreasoning and which show such a failure to recognise the validity of their demands'. She dismissed government claims that the civil rights movement was just a front for the IRA or far left agitators:

> What is happening is the product of a mass movement and an odd communist here and an odd Republican there cannot colour the

nature of this particular people's movement. It is a people's revolution and must be taken cognisance of. It is wrong to attempt to push it aside as being something invented by undesirable elements. If he really believes that, he has his head hopelessly in the sand. He must get it out or somebody must get his head out of the sand.[8]

On 22 November, under pressure now from London, Terence O'Neill announced a number of significant reforms – a points system to be used in allocating social housing, the replacement of Londonderry Corporation by an appointed Development Commission; an Ombudsman whose task would be to investigate citizens grievances; and a promise that the introduction of universal suffrage – 'one man, one vote' in local elections would be considered.'[9]

Just ten months after the Prime Minister had voted against Sheelagh's Bill, he was now preparing to concede much of what she had asked for. To extreme Loyalists O'Neill's reforms were a threat to 'our Constitution and Liberty.'[10] William Craig gave a speech which seemed to support Ulster declaring unilateral independence – not unlike Rhodesia in 1965. In parliament, Sheelagh asked O'Neill whether Craig's views in any way represented government policy and whether the reforms would go ahead. The Prime Minister's reply to her was: 'I want to make it clear that we mean business in implementing these proposals. This will be done effectively, objectively and as quickly as possible.'[11]

In a debate in Stormont on 15 October, Sheelagh again criticised the government for its handling of the crisis and reluctance to engage with the grievances of the minority community. 'I am an unrepentant parliamentary democrat. I believe that parliament should be the place to bring grievances, the place to have discussion, the place in which the problems of the people are ventilated and in an ideal situation, dealt with and solved.'[12]

Turning to the claim that the complaints made by the civil rights marchers were exaggerated, Sheelagh stated,

> It is true there is exaggeration but what case has ever been made which has not led to a degree of exaggeration? The fact that exaggeration exists is absolutely no excuse for trying to deny the existence of the problem.

> Everything I stand for, everything that has brought me to this house, is a demand to break away from traditional sectional attitudes. I want to see the two sections of our community, as they have been defined and existed in the past, come together.

She went on to speak about 'the perfectly genuine anger and resentment on the minority side due to the lack of deeds.' She commended the words of the Prime Minister over the years but stated: 'Words must be followed by deeds if they are going to have any value at all, and this is the cause of the anger – the justifiable anger – on the minority side.'

Criticising the government for politicising the police and for permitting violent loyalist counter-demonstrations, Sheelagh told parliament:

> The government must show that it is prepared to distinguish between demonstrations aimed at putting forward a point of view and those designed to prevent freedom of expression. What the vast majority of people in Northern Ireland want is a new normality based on justice. The government must have the courage to see that they get it.[13]

On 9 December, O'Neill made a television broadcast in which he warned that Ulster was 'at the crossroads.' He echoed the concerns which Sheelagh had so often expressed about Northern Ireland's standing in the world, asking viewers 'what kind of Ulster do you want?' Ulster could be either a 'happy respected province' or a 'political outcast.' He pledged that the reforms would be implemented, telling the civil rights supporters, 'your voice has been heard and clearly heard'.[14] Two days later he dismissed Craig from government. The speech was warmly welcomed and seemed to mark a new beginning or as Sheelagh declared: 'I believe that what we are seeing is the birth of a new era of justice.'

However, in January 1969, a march from Belfast to Derry by hard left members of the mainly student People's Democracy, who believed that O'Neill's reforms were 'too little, too late', led to renewed violence, as the Loyalists attacked the marchers and the police failed to protect them. Sectarian tensions now began to erupt and street protests escalated. O'Neill was now under pressure from both sides. On 28 January 1969 there was a debate in Stormont on the status of

Northern Ireland within the United Kingdom. Sheelagh spoke in the debate, in what would be her last major contribution in parliament. She stated that, with the rise of Scottish and Welsh nationalism and talk of regional devolution in England, the United Kingdom looked to be moving towards federalism and Northern Ireland needed to take account of these constitutional changes (changes the Liberals supported) and not imagine that the constitution of Northern Ireland would necessarily remain unchanged for ever in 'The New United Kingdom.'

She returned then to the question of reforms within Northern Ireland and what had to be done:

> The only way of ensuring that Northern Ireland is an acceptable part of the United Kingdom is to ensure that the voice of all the people here is heard and that the legitimate demands of a substantial section are acceded to. There is no weakness in listening to people's demands, listening to their point of view. The demands which have been highlighted in such vivid fashion in recent months are perfectly legitimate demands from any section of the community in any civilised country anywhere in the world.[15]

She went on to deal once more with how Northern Ireland was perceived – accusing the extreme loyalists of creating a situation where 'the majority of people in Great Britain' will 'want to have nothing more to do with us.' To outsiders, the province was seen as 'at best' a place which had to be tidied up from outside and at worst a 'place which should be discarded.' Sheelagh hoped that the Prime Minister would be able 'to redeem this unfortunate reputation we have acquired.' She was in no doubt as to what needed to happen:

> We must take the high ground to ensure that no person in this country, no matter what his creed or his political beliefs may be, has his rights as a citizen in any way diminished. It should be remembered that rights include the right of recourse to the law for remedy when an individual challenges rights or denies rights. One cannot say that a person has equal rights with others, unless, if that right is intruded upon, he has a remedy under the law.
>
> If we are going to take the right turn at the crossroads there must be a commitment to a specific course of action and an acknowledgement

that all those who feel they are suffering injustice will be given the necessary remedies to ensure that nobody is entitled to claim in the future that they have suffered injustice. The government must be prepared to make up the leeway which has accrued over the years in putting one section of the community at a disadvantage in relation to the other.[16]

She noted that Northern Ireland would continue to have within it 'people who think that the right and proper thing to do is to try and do down their opponents.' This being the case, 'One must have a system in place which ensures that attempts to do people down are open to remedy under law.'[17] A Unionist MP had suggested during the debate that Catholics should accept the Union Jack flag and the Queen. Sheelagh disagreed:

> Surely we can get to the stage where we can recognise that people are entitled to their own particular point of view. Let us try to get to the stage of accepting people as they are, respecting their views and insisting only on the one thing we are entitled to insist on, which is that the majority opinion of the people is to be the deciding factor in any decision we make on what is called the Constitutional issue.[18]

She concluded by referring to the 'Lunatic Fringe' of loyalism:

> There are people who still stick to the spirit of the old slogan 'A Protestant parliament for a Protestant people.' This ghost has to be laid firmly and to vanish from the scene forever. The only way this can be done is by taking positive action. There is no weakness in giving in to demands when those demands are legitimate.'[19]

She hoped that the people of the province would have 'at least the best government that is possible in the circumstances.' She believed that the majority of people in Northern Ireland wanted 'a country in which justice is evident and available to everybody and of which they can be proud.'[20]

On 3 February 1969 Terence O'Neill called a snap election in order to try and strengthen his position. With the dissolution of parliament, the Queen's University seat was abolished and Sheelagh had to find a new constituency. At first she wanted to run against William Craig in Larne. *The Guardian* reported:

The most heroic lost cause in the Ulster election goes to Sheelagh Murnaghan, a Roman Catholic who is standing as a Liberal against William Craig at Larne. 'I am going for the man who has caused most trouble in Northern Ireland', she says. Sheelagh is a brisk, middle-aged woman who twice captained the Irish Women's Hockey team. When she won the Stormont By-Election in 1961, she was Northern Ireland's first Liberal MP, the only woman at the bar and the only woman on the opposition benches. In Stormont she introduced four Human Rights Bills. The last, she says was modelled on the Race Relations Act – she just slipped in the word creed as well as race and colour.[21]

However, Sheelagh did not after all stand against the former Home Affairs Minister, because the Liberals did not want to split the anti-Unionist vote. Instead she stood in North Down – now part of the UK constituency in which she had gained 21.5 per cent of the vote in 1966. In her election literature she put herself and the Liberals forward as the voice of moderation.

> Northern Ireland has no future unless the old hatred between Protestant and Catholic comes to an end. Bigotry, suspicion and mistrust must be removed from our community. The main aim of the Liberal Party is to end these divisions. What Northern Ireland needs is widespread support for a Party composed of people from all creeds and classes dedicated to work together for the common good. This is what the Liberal Party is.

She also declared that she wanted to 'continue to fight for basic human rights for all classes and creeds. Equal pay and opportunity for women. A more mature attitude to Britain and to the Republic of Ireland.' She promised voters that 'if you elect me, I shall not be idle.'[22] However, the voice of moderation had now been drowned out by the tribal drumbeat. Sheelagh won just 1,567 votes (14.8 per cent). Her Unionist opponent took 9,013 votes (85 per cent). In Londonderry City, however, her party colleague, Claude Wilton, again polled well, coming within 700 votes of taking the seat. In the absence of a Catholic candidate, he attracted Catholic support with the memorable slogan 'Vote for Claude – the Catholic Prod.' In June he would succeed Sheelagh as the Liberal Party standard bearer in Stormont, when he was elected to the Senate.[23]

In the *Northern Radical* – the newsletter of the Ulster Liberals, the party Chairman, John Quinn, paid tribute to Sheelagh's work as an MP. 'I would like to compliment the tremendous work done at Stormont by our former MP, Sheelagh Murnaghan, who succeeded in getting a tremendous amount of publicity over the years for injecting sanity and common sense into the many difficult situations which have arisen.'[24]

Unfortunately sanity and common sense were now in very short supply in Northern Ireland. Marches and counter-marches fanned the flames of communal hatred, as *The Sunday Times* commented: 'The monster of sectarian violence is well out of its cage, the issue is now whether the state should exist and who should have the power.'[25]

On 17 April 1969 in a by-election for the Mid-Ulster seat at Westminster, Bernadette Devlin, a 21-year-old Catholic, from Tyrone who was a Queen's University student and a member of People's Democracy, stood as a 'Unity candidate' and was elected with over 33,000 votes. By 'Unity' was meant Catholic or Nationalist unity. The area had once been represented by George Murnaghan. Sheelagh rather admired her at first and sought to try and get her to moderate her views, believing that she needed guidance, but eventually came to see her as too extreme.[26] She was the second youngest woman ever elected to Westminster and her fiery rhetoric in parliament damning the Unionist government put more pressure on O'Neill to make reforms. He conceded universal suffrage – 'one man, one vote' – in local elections, but this concession infuriated right-wing Unionists. A loyalist Ulster Volunteer Force (UVF) bombing campaign was the final blow and the Prime Minister resigned, to be replaced by his cousin, James Chichester-Clark.[27]

As the political situation deteriorated, Albert McElroy, speaking at the General Assembly of the Non-Subscribing Presbyterian Church of Ireland in June, expressed his fear of where the country was heading. 'The situation is fraught with great danger. Things could easily return to the tragic conditions of the 20s and 30s.' As usual, the innocent, the ordinary people on both sides would pay the price and a new legacy of hatred created.[28] A few weeks later major violence erupted in Derry, Belfast and elsewhere. Over a number of days, ten people were killed, nearly 1,000 injured, thousands driven from their houses and the British Army had to be deployed on the streets. The 'Troubles' had begun.

Recently retired Liberal leader Jo Grimond in Belfast with
Julie Quinn, Berkley Farr and Sheelagh Murnaghan MP (1967)

In the aftermath of the rioting and the troop deployment, the British Home Secretary, James Callaghan, visited Northern Ireland to assess the situation. He met representatives of political parties and community groups. The Liberal delegation who met with him included Sheelagh. They recommended the need for further legislation against religious and political discrimination, keeping the army on the streets till all unrest had clearly ceased, the reintroduction of PR, the abolition of the Special Powers Act and the introduction of measures to combat intimidation. They also sought the transfer of housing allocation to a National Housing Association and reform of the Senate.[29]

The Cameron Commission headed by Lord Justice Cameron, which had been set up to investigate the causes of the violence from October 1968 onwards and to examine evidence for discrimination, published its findings on 12 September. While critical of the actions of some civil rights leaders, its report pointed the finger of blame mainly at the Unionist government and the police. The report accepted that the discrimination and disadvantage which Sheelagh had highlighted and sought to end did indeed exist. Further reforms were announced, including the setting up of a new Northern Ireland Housing Authority and the disarming of the RUC. A Ministry of Community Relations was set up and a Commission appointed to work with the Ministry. Sheelagh was a member of the Commission.[30]

At the Liberal Party assembly at Brighton in September, there was a special debate on Northern Ireland. Richard Moore, who was a prominent member of the party and had been Liberal candidate in North Antrim in 1966, welcomed the Cameron Report and condemned the Unionist government. The Liberals passed a resolution recognising 'the moral, legal and practical responsibility of the Westminster parliament to maintain civilised standards of government in all parts of the UK.' Moore backed up Sheelagh's argument that 'The Government of Ireland Act made no provision for Human Rights in the North.'

He pointed out that the Cameron Report had 'endorsed everything the Northern Ireland Liberal Party had said in the past and, in accepting the Report, the Northern Ireland government have conceded our case.' He also reminded the Assembly of 'the attempts of Miss Sheelagh Murnaghan to introduce a Bill of Rights at Stormont, only to have it thrown out 4 times by the Unionists.'[31] The leader of the Liberals, Jeremy Thorpe, also addressed the issue of Northern Ireland during his speech to the assembly.

> If only the Ulster government had accepted the Human Rights Bills, attacking extremism, which were presented on at least four occasions by the then Liberal MP, Miss Sheelagh Murnaghan, they could have begun to win the confidence of the Catholic minority and it would have been very much more difficult for the extremists to exploit the situation.[32]

Notes

1   Gordon Gillespie, 'The Ulster Liberal Party 1956–1973',
       MSSc thesis (Queen's University Belfast, 1984), p. 103.
2   Ibid., pp 60–61.

3   Gordon Gillespie, *Albert McElroy: The Radical Minister1915–1975* (Belfast, 1985), p. 26.
4   Jonathan Bardon, *A History of Ulster* (Belfast, 1992), p. 652.
5   *Irish Press,* 10 Oct. 1968.
6   Northern Ireland House of Commons Reports, vol. 70, cols 1828–34 (15 Oct. 1968).
7   Ibid., col. 1832.
8   Ibid., cols 1830–31.
9   Bardon, *History of Ulster*, p. 657.
10 Ibid.
11 NIHC, vol. 70, col. 2115 (24 Dec. 1968).
12 Ibid., cols 1005–06 (15 Oct. 1968).
13 Ibid., col. 2180.
14 Bardon, *History of Ulster*, p. 658.
15 NIHC, vol. 71, col. 479 (28 Jan. 1969).
16 Ibid., col. 483.
17 Ibid., col. 484.
18 Ibid.
19 Ibid., col. 485.
20 Ibid.
21 *The Guardian*, 7 Feb. 1969.
22 Election Address 1969, General Election, ULP Papers, PRONI, D2951 (see also D3342).
23 Gillespie, 'The Ulster Liberal Party', p. 65.
24 *Northern Radical*, no. 18 (April/May 1969).
25 Bardon, *History of Ulster*, p. 664.
26 Interview with Maurice Hayes by Nick McGinley, (nephew of Sheelagh Murnaghan) DVD (2004).
27   Bardon, *History of Ulster*, p. 664.
28 Gillespie, *Albert McElroy*, pp 20–28.
29 Gillespie, 'The Ulster Liberal Party', p. 67.
30 Ibid., p. 68.
31 Ibid.
32 Ibid., p. 69.

Sheelagh Murnaghan and Berkley Farr during the 1973 election for the first Northern Ireland Assembly (*Belfast Telegraph*)

8

After Stormont

SHEELAGH MURNAGHAN HAD CONTINUED her legal work during her parliamentary career and was a member of the Incorporated Council of Law Reporting for Northern Ireland. She was the only woman on the council and, as the sixties drew to a close, she was still the only practising female barrister at the Northern Ireland Bar. It was not until December 1971 that a second woman, Philomena Bateson, was called to the Bar. Thereafter the numbers began to increase. In 1974, for example, three women became barristers including a future Irish President, Mary McAleese, and Eilis McDermott, who would become Northern Ireland's first female QC.

But for most of Sheelagh's legal career, there was, as one male QC acknowledged, 'an endemic gender problem'[1] in the Northern Irish legal world. It was also still a strongly Protestant world, although the number of Catholics would gradually increase. Sheelagh was also appointed in the summer of 1969 to chair an employment appeals tribunal. She would chair many such tribunals in the years to come hearing cases with common-sense and compassion. She would arrive for work carrying bundles of documents in one hand and a dog in the other. Sheelagh had a deep love for dogs and had several of them.

The Community Relations Ministry had been set up by Prime Minister Chichester-Clark as part of the reform agenda. The first Minister for Community Relations was a moderate Unionist, David Simpson. In November 1969, an Act of Parliament set up the Community Relations Commission to support the work of the Ministry. The Commission sought to tackle sectarianism by 'instituting a community development programme aimed at bringing together the Protestant and Catholic working class.' The Commission was empowered 'to develop and secure the adoption of educational programmes included to eliminate or discourage discriminatory practices.' The Commission could also 'establish services for giving advice on community relations to local and other bodies or persons' and 'could provide or arrange for the provision of training courses in connection with community relations.'[2] The first Chairman of the Community Relations Commission was Maurice Hayes, a senior civil servant and a Catholic; he would later serve as Northern Ireland's Ombudsman and subsequently as a member of the Senate in the Republic. Hayes admired Sheelagh's strong sense of justice, compassion and her efforts to make the Commission a real agent for change. In his memoirs, Hayes recalled how:

> On the first Christmas after the inception of the Commission, Sheelagh proposed, and the rest of us weakly agreed, that we should show ourselves to the Belfast Citizenry by a tour of pubs along the so-called peaceline. Sheelagh leading the way – respectable middle aged men in business suits and Bessie Maconachie [former Unionist MP for Queen's] into pub after crowded pub, shamefacedly introducing ourselves to the drinking public who, momentarily released from the stress of conflict in seasonal revelry, could not care less who we were.

Sheelagh thought it had been 'an excellent effort'.[3] Hayes recalled Sheelagh affectionately as a 'slightly eccentric figure' who 'still retained some of the aggressiveness of her no-nonsense style of (hockey) play. She dressed in rather butch tweeds and smoked manikins, and was not afraid to tackle anyone in debate.'

Hayes regarded her as 'one of the few truly liberal voices around', with 'a tremendous heart.' He was critical of her public speaking abilities – considering that she could be 'appalling convoluted and imprecise' and could also be 'a woolly thinker' and 'confused activity with action.' But he admired the lengths she would go to help people. In his memoirs, he recounted a story of an occasion when Sheelagh drove down to Newry with a Traveller and spent the whole day helping him to secure a £10 reduction in the price of a van. 'When I pointed out that in much less time in the Bar Library, she could have earned £20, paid the Traveller his £10 and saved herself a lot of time and trouble, she seemed to think I had missed the point, maybe I had.'[4] In an interview in 2004 with her nephew Nick McGinley, Hayes called Sheelagh 'a beacon of good sense who was ahead of her time and a benchmark for society.'[5]

In his obituary notice for Sheelagh, Hayes echoed the words of Jeremy Thorpe.

> She had a vision of a Northern Ireland where Catholics and Protestants could live and work in peace together under the Rule of Law. Her voice in the sixties was one of the few publicly and consistently to challenge injustice and had it been listened to and modest reforms introduced, much subsequent pain and suffering might have been avoided.[6]

Sheelagh served on the Community Relations Commission for three years. Community development was at the core of the Commission's work and 16 Community Development Officers were trained up. The hope was that the communities with which the officers and the Commission worked would through support and self-help, 'increase its own self-esteem and self-confidence and on the basis of this confidence would develop the desire to look outside itself and find areas of common interest with other communities.' The officers liaised with local community leaders, associations, etc.

The Commission also gave some support to existing cross-community groups such as PACE (Protestant and Catholic Encounter), and Women Together. Many of these organisations concentrated on 'actual personal relationships.' As Northern Ireland society fell apart, and Sheelagh's vision of a country in which Catholic and Protestant would live in peace and mutual respect became a fast receding dream, such encounters were important. 'Simply getting together – being seen with the other side becomes a significant gesture in a divided society.'

However, the Commission never managed to achieve what it was hoping to do. The government had set it up in haste as part of the reform package after the August 1969 violence. The NICRC Director, Hywel Griffiths, a Welsh academic, had a vision for community relations which was way too radical for a government which, Griffiths felt, had hoped the Commission would 'quell unrest with modest reform' and, win Catholic support for the State' – not as Griffiths wanted, 'a radical campaign to encourage self-confidence and solidarity among the disaffected sections of the population' – an aim which Sheelagh largely shared.[7] There was also a lack of interest among the public. A conference for schools organised by the CRC held in Omagh in 1970 was attended by just 30 pupils from six schools – invitations had been sent out to 38 schools.[8]

The Community Relations Ministry was underfunded and went through five ministers in five years. David Bleakley of the Labour Party was in the job just six months. In October 1971, Gerald Newe, a senior civil servant from County Antrim who was a co-founder and Vice-Chairman of PACE, became the first Catholic to serve as a government minister in the 50 years of Northern Ireland, when he was appointed Minister of State in the Ministry. But again this was little more than gesture politics at the time when most Nationalist politicians were disengaging from the state.

In February 1972, the government turned down the budget requested by the Commission. Maurice Hayes resigned in protest at government security policy and increasing alienation of Catholics. Hywel Griffiths left soon afterwards. The UK government's imposition of direct rule ended the Ministry, although the Commission survived another two years. By then disillusion and demoralisation had set in. The Commission was finally dissolved in 1975 and its functions absorbed into the Department of Education (Northern Ireland). Many of the programmes the Commission had hoped to develop also had to be postponed because of the escalating violence.

As the province exploded in mayhem after the introduction of internment Sheelagh and her colleagues found themselves 'providing emergency relief during the greatest population movement in Europe since the Second World War.' The Commission was also 'documenting and responding with assistance to the effects of government oppressive security policy' – again something not to the liking of the government.[9] Sheelagh was asked by many women for help to get their husbands or sons released from army custody during this time.

The Troubles had begun to escalate within weeks of the setting up of the Commission. Sheelagh herself was a victim of the violence when, on the evening of 8 February 1970, her home in Windsor Avenue, Belfast was bombed. She was out at the time and apart from blowing out a door and windows, little major damage was done. Sheelagh's response was simple; 'I will not be bombed out of my home'.[10] She cleared up the broken glass and rubble and went to bed. The perpetrators were never identified and Sheelagh kept an open mind.

Her defence of the New Public Order (Amendment) Act which it was believed would replace the Special Powers Act, could have made her an IRA target, but it was most likely that the attack was the responsibility of the UVF. A number of other politicians were targeted by the UVF at this time. One was Austin Currie; another was Ulster Unionist Richard Ferguson; another was a close friend of Sheelagh's – Anne Dickson, who had been a strong critic of discrimination while serving as a Unionist Councillor in Carrick and was continuing Sheelagh's work in calling for reform since her election in February 1969 to Stormont. In 1977 Mrs Dickson would become the first woman to lead a political party in Northern Ireland when she became head of the Unionist Party of Northern Ireland.[11]

By the summer of 1970 the Provisional and Official IRAs had begun their military campaigns. The British army alienated Catholic opinion through heavy-handed security measures and loyalist paramilitaries were also active. Against this background community polarisation grew, with Catholics and Protestants fleeing to the comfort of their own areas. This atmosphere was disastrous for the Liberal Party. In the Westminster general election of June 1970, the party did very badly – securing only a third of the vote that they had received in 1966, when they had one fewer candidate.[12] The Liberals were also losing ground to new political parties. Albert McElroy wrote in despair about how 'Northern Ireland produced more political parties in a month than most other countries in a century.'[13]

The new parties included the Social Democratic and Labour Party, founded by Gerry Fitt, John Hume and Austin Currie, and the Alliance Party of Northern Ireland (APNI), led by former Liberal member, Oliver Napier. Alliance was particularly dangerous to the Liberals because not only did it take votes from Catholics but they could get support from Protestants due to the fact that unlike the Liberals, the party emphasised its support of the Union with Britain. Many Catholic Liberals who favoured a united Ireland at some point now went to the SDLP. A survey of the Liberals carried out by Berkley Farr in 1967 had shown the Liberals to be a largely middle class party whose membership was approximately 42 per cent Protestant, 35 per cent Catholic, 17 per cent non-religious/humanist and 3 per cent Jewish.[14] Now many of the Protestants too began to leave. Albert McElroy was deeply hurt at the defections. Sheelagh, however, elected to stay.

The violence was now beginning to claim the lives of her friends and acquaintances. In December 1971, Senator Jack Barnhill of the Ulster Unionists was murdered at his Strabane home by the Official IRA.[15] In March 1972, Ann Owens, a member of the Belfast Young Liberals, was killed along with another woman in the Provisional IRA bombing of the Abercorn Restaurant. She had only just recovered from injuries received in an IRA bomb attack on her workplace the previous October.[16]

The introduction of internment in August 1971 by the new Northern Ireland Prime Minister, Brian Faulkner worried and angered Sheelagh. 'Such a wholesale violation of human rights ran counter to everything Murnaghan stood for, both as a Liberal and as a barrister,' according to Anne Dickson. Sheelagh 'gave up her favourite vices of cigars and brandy for the duration,' as a protest.[17] She lobbied British ministers to have the system ended.

The introduction of internment and the failure of the government to have an inquiry into the army killing of two civilians in Derry led to the SDLP and many other Nationalists withdrawing from Stormont and county councils. The SDLP set up an alternative assembly in Dungiven. The Liberals continued to engage with the government, however, seeing no advantage for Catholics in withdrawing and leaving the government with no Catholic/Nationalist voices to question and engage with them. The Liberals put forward a number of proposals for the governance of Northern Ireland including a revamped council system in which there would be 12 councils elected by PR, a 75-seat Northern Ireland Assembly, also elected by PR and a new system for elections to Westminster under which the province would become a single 12-seat constituency – again using PR – rather similar to Sheelagh's old Queen's constituency.[18]

In March 1972, direct rule was introduced to Northern Ireland and Stormont suspended. The new Northern Ireland Secretary of State, William Whitelaw, came to Belfast with his ministerial and civil service. As he later recalled 'the whole place was in uproar'.[19] To try and learn what was happening and what needed to be done, Whitelaw set up an 11-member advisory commission in May. The commission comprised seven Protestants and four Catholics.[20] There were two women appointed and one was Sheelagh. In an interview she stated that Whitelaw needed to be given a chance – 'it was essential for people to co-operate with Mr. Whitelaw's administration'. She felt unable to say what success she felt the commission would have but said she was adopting a 'wait and see attitude.'[21] Her appointment was welcomed by the *Northern Radical*:

> Those of us who are concerned about the future of this province can only have been encouraged by the announcement that she is to serve on Mr. Whitelaw's commission. He knows she would not have accepted the post if she did not think that the commission would play a crucial role in bringing peace to the community, and our faith in Mr. Whitelaw can only have been increased by his making such a sensible choice.[22]

Unionists criticised the commission as a group of well-meaning middle class moderates who were 'unable to give advice.' But the Commission was able to give Whitelaw some guidance and to suggest ways forward. For Sheelagh, membership of the commission put her 'in a position to stress the needs for reforms which Liberals had long proposed.' A Liberal delegation which met with Whitelaw on 23 May, recommended a change in Northern Ireland's constitution to ensure a 'community or power-sharing government.[23] PR was essential for Northern Ireland because it would 'break down the polarised political situation.' They felt that PR would help end sectarianism in local politics.

In papers presented to the Secretary of State in September, ahead of multiparty talks in Darlington, the Liberals again suggested using a departmental committee system elected by PR from among assembly members. Issues such as security and judicial appointments should remain with London. An idea first put forward by Sheelagh a decade earlier – joint RUC and Garda patrols in certain border areas was again suggested. There was also a Liberal suggestion that Northern Ireland's position in the UK could be best secured by making a change in the constitutional position of the province dependant on a referendum in which the people of Northern Ireland would decide their destiny. At a further meeting with Whitelaw in December the Liberals put forward one further proposal – a Bill of Rights to guarantee civil rights in Northern Ireland.[24]

For almost a decade, Sheelagh had ploughed a lonely furrow trying to get such a Bill passed. Now everyone began to jump on the bandwagon. 'The Alliance Party wanted a Bill of Rights guaranteeing to all citizens their fundamental Human Rights based on the Universal Declaration of Human Rights', and put this idea forward at the Darlington talks. The Ulster Unionists who had repeatedly dismissed Sheelagh's Bills now proposed 'the introduction of a precise and comprehensive Bill of Rights.'[25]

When William Whitelaw published his White Paper for the proposed future government of Northern Ireland in March 1973, the proposals included a Charter of Human Rights for the province. 'The proposals from the UK government had been a result of the Darlington Conference but had also been shaped by his Advisory Commission of which Sheelagh was a member.'[26]

The proposed charter focused on the issues of equality and discrimination and would encompass 'the right to equality of benefit and opportunity.' 'Any action of a discriminatory character by a government, a local authority or public body could be made the subject of a Court action' and there would be 'a whole range of legal remedies.' The White Paper stated: 'There has been a general agreement that a new settlement should in some way or other make provision for the protection of fundamental Human Rights and Freedoms.'[27] One weakness of the proposed Charter was that it 'lacked proposals for process rights and emergency powers.'[28]

During her time on the commission, Sheelagh continued to press for the end of internment. In February 1973, Whitelaw permitted the commission to visit the Maze Prison, where many of the internees were being held. Sheelagh expressed concern that 'the present parole arrangements are now strict, as to amount to inhumanity.'

As the government prepared to publish the White Paper setting out its proposal for devolved government, Sheelagh wrote a piece for the *Northern Radical*.

> Whatever scheme is put forward for Northern Ireland's future, one thing is certain, and that is that the 'All-or-nothing boys' on both sides will try to oppose it. It is inevitable therefore that there will be a real risk of continuing violence, but the risk will be less if the British government adopts a firm 'take it or leave it' attitude in respect of the new outline proposals. The outline scheme must take cognisance on the one hand of the fact that both the Republic and Northern Ireland are now members of the E.E.C., and on the other of the emotional and other factors which render impractical the political unification of

Ireland. It must concern itself very deeply with complex problems of identity; it must recognise that Northern Ireland has achieved a separate and distinct identity over the years. It must, in effect, confer statehood on Northern Ireland with a view to creating what could be called the 'Association of Irish States.' It would be nonsensical to contemplate complete independence for Northern Ireland but the aim should be to gradually achieve as much devolution of power as soon as possible, and to do it as soon as possible.

The form of the Northern Ireland state must be such that all its citizens can identify with it, whatever their religious or political views. This was impossible in the past when government was permanently in the hands of one section. The new system must ensure that such power as there is should be accessible for all sections of the community. The exact details of how this is to be achieved should be open to negotiation, but the basic principle must be a pre-condition of any power being devolved at all. If there is to be a Council of Ireland, it must have some real function, and the most practical function it could have would be to tackle the Social and Economic development of the Border counties. These counties should be declared a special development area, and the area should be to achieve a situation in which responsibility for the new area would be jointly accepted by Northern Ireland and the Republic. Jointly appointed Commissions should be set up immediately for the Foyle-Valley and the Newry area and these commissions should be given very full powers and adequate resources. The powers should be sufficiently extensive as to enable the RUC and Garda operating jointly within it. Recruits from Northern Ireland could, if they wished, join the Garda rather than the RUC and vice versa. Within the zone the joint force would be responsible to the Council of Ireland through the local Commission.

The actual territory within the zone would remain part of Northern Ireland or the Republic, as at present, and would continue to elect representatives to the respective legislatures but the Council of Ireland would have all responsibilities. For the time being Westminster must retain all responsibility for security in Northern Ireland as a whole, but as soon as possible the responsibility should be transferred to the new legislative Assembly. One of the most urgent necessities is the restoration of confidence in the police. There can be no substitute for the RUC. People must be made to see how terribly unfair it was to blame the police force as a whole for the faults of a few and for the deficiencies of the system under which they had to operate in the past.

The whole emphasis of policy from now on should be directed to making the people of Northern Ireland realise how interdependent they are on each other. If any oath of allegiance it to be required in the future it should be an oath of allegiance to the people of Northern Ireland. In other words to the community as a whole. Loyalty to the community is something which the community is entitled to demand and which all should be prepared to give.[29]

The White Paper was published in early March 1973 and proposed the creation of a 78-seat devolved Assembly elected by PR, a power-sharing executive and a council of Ireland – consisting of bodies overseeing cross-border cooperation in socio-economic areas such as tourism, transport and regional development. The White Paper proposals contained much of what Sheelagh and her colleagues had sought for so many years. In June, elections took place to the Northern Ireland Assembly. For the last time in her career, Sheelagh ran for election, in South Belfast.

The Liberals were well satisfied with the White Paper and campaigned in support of the proposed power-sharing agreement. In her election literature, Sheelagh also condemned the violence on both sides which continued to blight the province: 'No cause, however sincere, could justify the kind of deeds which have been done here, no cause, whether it be the unification of Ireland or the preservation of Ulster is furthered by opening the flood gates of evil.'[30]

The elections proved disastrous for the Liberals. Sheelagh got only 548 votes and came in eighteenth out of 19 candidates in South Belfast, while Berkley Farr also did very badly in South Down. Both candidates lost their deposits.[31]

'The year 1973 effectively marked the end of the era in which the Liberals played an important part in the politics of Northern Ireland.' The local government elections to the new 26 district councils, held in May were also very bad for the party. However, the Constitution of Northern Ireland Act (1973), which brought the new institutions of government into force in July, did reflect the Liberal vision of how the province should be run. Section 20 of the Act was particularly significant in reflecting Sheelagh's human rights agenda. It created the Standing Advisory Commission on Human Rights (SACHR), which

... was charged with (a) advising the Secretary of State on the adequacy and effectiveness of the current law in preventing discrimination on grounds of religious belief or political views and in providing redress for persons aggrieved by discrimination on either grounds, and (b) keeping the Secretary of State informed as to the extent to which public authorities have prevented discrimination on either grounds.

The Standing Advisory Commission was only the second national human rights institution founded anywhere in the world (France had set up a similar body in 1947).[32] The first chairman of the Commission was British Trade Union leader, Lord Vic Feather. He and his successor, Lord Plant, 'quickly decided to see whether a Bill of Rights for Northern Ireland should be put in place for Northern Ireland'. The Constitution Act also saw another of Sheelagh's campaigns realised when capital punishment was abolished in Northern Ireland. The last man sentenced to death in Northern Ireland was Liam Holden from Belfast, convicted of the murder of a British soldier in 1972. Whitelaw reprieved him in April 1973. Holden spent 16 years in prison. His conviction was quashed in 2012.[33]

The Sunningdale Agreement between the British and Irish governments, the SDLP, Alliance Party and some Ulster Unionists set up the power-sharing executive. The Sunningdale Agreement was welcomed by the Liberals. Sheelagh was, however, unenthusiastic about the Council of Ireland, which, as proposed at Sunningdale, would have much more remit than she had envisaged in her article on the White Paper. 'She saw it as offering little more than the possibility of economic and security co-operation. She feared that raising the border issue risked undermining Unionist support for power sharing.'[34]

Sheelagh's fears about the Council of Ireland were justified as a majority of Unionists opposed it and, in a British general election in February 1974, won 11 of the 12 seats with a fraction over 50 per cent of the total vote undermining the newly established power-sharing executive. Liberals had advocated the introduction of PR for the 12 Westminster seats. There was also a court case brought against the agreement in the Republic by former minister Kevin Boland, in which he argued that the agreement violated the Irish Constitution – which claimed sovereignty over Northern Ireland, and undermined the rights of Irish citizens living in Northern Ireland.

The case was heard in the High Court by George Murnaghan, a cousin of Sheelagh's. Dismissing Mr Boland's case, Mr Justice Murnaghan ruled that a declaration by the Irish government in the

Sunningdale Agreement communiqué acknowledging that the status of Northern Ireland could only change, if and when a majority of the people of Northern Ireland consented to such change, was 'no more than a statement of policy by the government' and did not violate the Constitution. He also dismissed the argument put forward by Boland that the Agreement imposed British citizenship and nationality on Irish citizens in Northern Ireland, 'It does nothing of the sort.' Judge Murnaghan stated: 'I am far from convinced that this court should concern itself with a declaration of policy by the government which in itself cannot affect the legal rights of any citizen.'[35]

The Northern Ireland Executive, weakened by Unionist opposition, finally collapsed in May following the Ulster Workers Council strike. In May 1975 a Constitutional Convention was elected to try and work out a political settlement for the North. The Liberals did not put forward any candidates. Sheelagh's friend Anne Dickson was one of the 25 candidates of the pro-power-sharing Unionist Party of Northern Ireland candidates who were elected. The eight Alliance Party candidates elected included former Liberal Oliver Napier. During the Convention discussions the issue of a Human Rights Bill came up again. The Alliance Party pressed for 'a Bill of Rights in the future Constitution of Northern Ireland. Such a Bill of Rights must guarantee Equality of Citizenship to every person in the province.'[36]

The United Ulster Unionists also recommended 'A Bill of Constitutional Rights' to guarantee the stability and integrity of the Northern Ireland Constitution and a General Bill of Rights and duties to protect the rights of the individual citizen. The UUUC wanted such a Bill to be for the United Kingdom as a whole, however, not just for Northern Ireland.[37] The SDLP also considered the human rights issue and advocated making the European Convention on Human Rights part of domestic law in Northern Ireland. In 1976 the SACHR brought in Liberal barrister Anthony Lester QC and Anthony Donaldson to examine the question of having a Bill of Rights for Northern Ireland based on the European Convention on Human Rights. The proposals for a Bill of Rights got nowhere in the 1970s, but did show that the seed sown by Sheelagh a decade earlier was still there to be cultivated and that across the British and Irish political spectrum, the ideas for which she had campaigned were now gaining wide acceptance. One area where her ideas were put into law was the Fair

Employment Act (1976), described as 'possibly the most significant human rights development in Northern Ireland in the 1970s.'

The Fair Employment Act was, 'The first law anywhere in these islands to make religious and political discrimination unlawful in the private as well as the public sphere.' A Fair Employment Agency was set up to monitor the enforcement of the Act, with Bob Cooper of the Alliance Party (another friend of Sheelagh's) as its first CEO.[38]

The Advisory Commission to the Northern Ireland Secretary had been wound up following the Assembly elections in 1973, having held 86 meetings over 15 months and influenced the Constitution Act of 1973. Sheelagh remained active in many different organisations and committees during the 1970s. She was a member of cross-community organisations such as Protestant and Catholic Encounter (PACE) and Women Together. Her international outlook was reflected in her membership of the United Nations Association. She was a member of the Belfast District of Soroptimists, while a lifelong enthusiasm for cars (she owned an Austin A48) led her to join the Institute of Advanced Motorists Association. She remained strongly involved with the Liberal Party even as the party entered its decline, serving as convenor for the policy sub-committee. She contributed frequently to the *Northern Radical*. In July 1972, for example, she wrote:

> A political unification of Ireland is too remote a prospect to be considered as the basis for a solution at the present time. The campaign of violence, far from furthering the cause of a United Ireland, has served to postpone the gradual evolution in that direction which was taking place before the present upheaval started.

With regard to Northern Ireland, she wrote: 'In practice there could be no such thing as complete independence – but there is everything to be said for seeking to channel this desperate mood into a constructive desire for self reliance and a legitimate pride.' She described the IRA campaign as 'one of the saddest episodes in all our tragic Irish history, characterised as it has been by mindless violence and brutality.'[39]

In May 1970, Sheelagh Murnaghan and Berkley Farr met with Lord Crowther and his commission when they visited Northern Ireland and presented the Ulster Liberal Party view on the British Constitution and its future to the commission. Their proposals included the federalisation of the United Kingdom, with four devolved parliaments for the nations of the UK and a federal parliament at Westminster; a PR voting system and a Federal Bill of Rights enforced by parliament.[40]

Like most Liberals, Sheelagh was strongly supportive of the European Economic Community – as it was then known. At the end of 1962, she told the *Belfast Telegraph* that the event of the year which had given her the most pleasure was Britain's application to join the EEC.[41] She welcomed Britain's eventual accession in 1973 and, in 1975, she took part in the 'Northern Ireland for Europe' campaign during the referendum on Britain's EEC membership, which was held in June. She remained in close contact with the UK Liberal Party and served on the Advisory Group to assist the Liberal Party Northern Ireland spokesman, Alan Beith, during the late 1970s. The party leader, Jeremy Thorpe, greatly admired her and invited her to his wedding reception at Covent Garden Opera House in 1973 (she was unable to attend but was represented by Berkley Farr.)[42] When the Ulster Liberal leader, Albert McElroy died in March 1975, Sheelagh penned a moving tribute to him in *The Irish Times*. She and Albert had been great friends and she admired his love of politics, and his complete lack of bigotry, and his moral and physical courage:

> The only thing he found it really hard to forgive was inhumanity. The gross inhumanity of so many of the events of the past few years drove him almost to despair. It was not fear which made him recoil from the violence, much though he abhorred it. What almost destroyed him was the sheer evil of it all. That people could stoop to such deeds was beyond his comprehension. He was saddened also by his realisation that the unity of hearts and minds in Ireland, which he had always so deeply desired, was becoming more and more remote as horror was piled on horror.

She noted that Albert McElroy had feared that the civil rights campaign would eventually lead to violence. 'No one could have been happier than he if his forebodings had been proved wrong. In the result, he was proven right, and most of the joy went out of his life. Now he himself is gone from our lives. Ireland will be the poorer without him.'[43]

1985 book launch in Dunmurry of *Albert H. McElroy: The Radical Minister*, left to right: Berkley Farr, Rev. William McMillan, Sheelagh Murnaghan, Richard Moore, Gordon Gillespie (author) and Bishop, later Cardinal, Cahal Daly

The violence continued to claim the lives of acquaintances of Sheelagh during those terrible years. On 16 September 1974 – 'a black day for the legal profession in Northern Ireland',[44] Judge Rory Conaghan and Martin McBirney QC were murdered at their homes by the IRA. In March 1977, the Deputy Director for Public Prosecutions for County Down, Rory O'Kelly – who had been a prominent Civil Rights supporter, was murdered by the IRA in his native Coalisland. In January 1981, the man who had been Speaker of the Stormont House of Commons during Sheelagh's time there, Sir Norman Stronge, was murdered along with his son James at his County Armagh home by the IRA, in retaliation for the attempted murder of Bernadette Devlin by the UVF. Judge William Doyle was murdered by the IRA outside a Belfast church in January 1983. Sheelagh's home town of Omagh suffered repeated bombings and several killings.

The human rights of Travellers remained close to Sheelagh's heart in the years after she left parliament. She had helped start a school for Traveller children, St Paul's in Belfast, working as school treasurer for many years and helping to organise excursions for the pupils,[45] and worked closely with groups like the Assisi Fellowship in their outreach work with the Belfast Traveller community. In May 1972, a report in the *Belfast Telegraph* highlighted the work Sheelagh was doing for Travellers and others:

The Voice of Reason

Miss Sheelagh Murnaghan has shown unmistakeable courage in speaking out against the pressures that are being imposed on Catholics to persuade them to withdraw from public life. More than that, she has catalogued her reasons for declaring why she is against 'opting out' with a conviction what could only stem from a spirit that is both sincere and magnanimous. In present circumstances when life is so wantonly taken, the voice of a woman defying the tide and expressing the basic Christian doctrine of concern for her fellow human beings is not to go unnoticed by those who hold a different faith, or he can only hope, unheard by those of her own.

People like Miss Murnaghan and the Belfast Itinerants Settlement Committee are trying to do something to help. Last night Miss Murnaghan wrote an unemotional yet moving letter in the *Belfast Telegraph* outlining one of the latest problems. She was appealing for contributions to provide 'some sort of vehicle for a group of people trying to make ends meet by collecting scrap. 'A man cannot carry much on the wheels of an old pram.' Miss Murnaghan has long championed the cause of people in such a plight. In parliament and out, she has worked to make their burden lighter in the age of the affluent society and the welfare State. She is one of those who holds high something looked for – the torch of compassion.[46]

Fr Alec Reid, who worked with her for Travellers, recalled how Sheelagh was 'very down to earth' and prepared to go into the muddy caravan sites. The Travellers would refer to her affectionately as 'The Cigar Lady.'[47]

Sheelagh also kept in touch with Queen's University, serving as an elected member of the University's 60-strong governing body – the Senate. She retained her links with hockey as well. She occasionally refereed matches into the 1970s and was a life member of the Ulster Ladies Hockey Organisation.

In her campaigns for human rights legislation and for the abolition of the death penalty, Sheelagh had made a significant contribution to

Northern Ireland. But she also, as Constance Rynder has written 'made a unique contribution to the fight against gender discrimination in the workplace.'[48] In the 1980s Sheelagh heard the very first case of sexual harassment brought before a tribunal in the UK. 'The outcome of that case reverberated throughout not only the UK but also the whole European Community'.

Notes

1 Justine McCarthy: *Mary McAleese: The Outsider* (Dublin, 1999), p. 33.
2 https://cain.ulster.ac.uk/issues/community/index.html, accessed 14 May 2019.
3 Maurice Hayes, *Minority Verdict: Experiences of a Catholic Public Servant* (Belfast, 1995), p. 181.
4 Ibid., p. 181.
5 Interview with Maurice Hayes by Nick McGinley, (nephew of Sheelagh Murnaghan) DVD (2004).
6 Sheelagh Murnaghan Obituary: *The Independent*, 21 Sep. 1993.
7 https://cain.ulster.ac.uk/issues/community/index.html, accessed 14 May 2019.
8 Ibid.
9 https://cain.ulster.ac.uk/issues/community/index.html, accessed 18 June 2019.
10 *Irish Press*, 9 Feb. 1970.
11 Rynder, 'Sheelagh Murnaghan and the Struggle for Human Rights', p. 460, n. 37.
12 Gordon Gillespie, 'The Ulster Liberal Party 1956–1973', MSSc thesis (Queen's University Belfast, 1984), p. 71.
13 Gordon Gillespie, *Albert McElroy: The Radical Minister 1915–1975* (Belfast, 1985), p. 30.
14 Gillespie, 'The Ulster Liberal Party', p. 37.
15 David McKitterick, Seamus Kelters, Brian Feeney and Chris Thornton: *Lost Lives: The Stories of the Men, Women and Children Who Died as a Result of the Northern Ireland Troubles* (Edinburgh, 1999), pp 131, 161.
16 *Northern Radical*, Apr. 1972.
17 Rynder, 'Sheelagh Murnaghan and the Ulster Liberal Party', p. 19.
18 Gillespie, 'The Ulster Liberal Party', p. 73.

19 Jonathan Bardon, *A History of Ulster* (Belfast, 1992), p. 690.
20 *Irish Press*, 26 May 1972.
21 Ibid.
22 *Northern Radical*, June 1972.
23 Gillespie, 'The Ulster Liberal Party', pp 76–7.
24 Brice Dickson, *The European Convention on Human Rights and Conflict in Northern Ireland* (Oxford, 2012), p. 21.
25 Monica McWilliams, Anne Smyth and Priyamvada Yarnell, *Political Capacity Building: Advancing a Bill of Rights for Northern Ireland* (Belfast, 2014), p. 16.
26 Ibid., pp 18–19.
27 Dickson, *The European Convention on Human Rights*, p. 22.
28 Ibid.
29 *Northern Radical*, Feb. 1973.
30 Election address, Assembly elections, June 1973 (Private Papers, Berkley Farr).
31 Berkley Farr, 'Liberalism in Unionist Northern Ireland',
32 Dickson, *The European Convention on Human Rights*, p. 22.
33 https://en.wikipedia.org/wiki/Capital_punishment_in_the_United_Kingdom, accessed 14 May 2019.
34 Rynder, 'Sheelagh Murnaghan and the Ulster Liberal Party', p. 17.
35 See *Irish Independent*, 17 Jan. 1974.
36 Dickson, *The European Convention on Human Rights*, p. 24.
37 Ibid., p. 24.
38 Ibid.
39 *Northern Radical*, July 1972,
40 Ibid., no. 24, June 1970.
41 *Belfast Telegraph*, 29 Dec. 1962.
42 Conversation with Berkley Farr, July 2017.
43 *Northern Radical*, June 1975.
44 *Irish Independent*, 17 Sep. 1974.
45 Interview with Maurice Hayes and Fr Alec Reid by Nick McGinley, (nephew of Sheelagh Murnaghan) DVD (2004).
46 *Belfast Telegraph*, 26 May 1972.
47 Interview with Fr Alec Reid, by Nick McGinley, DVD (2004).
48 Rynder, 'Sheelagh Murnaghan and the Struggle for Human Rights', p. 447.

9

Advancing Rights for Women

SHEELAGH MURNAGHAN DID NOT see herself as a feminist. She had been brought up and educated to see herself as the equal of men. Equality was something for which she campaigned throughout her life – equality for the Catholic community in Northern Ireland, equality for the Travellers. Equality for women in the workplace was just another strand of her campaign to make her country a place where men and women regardless of creed, colour or social class had equal rights and equal opportunities in a society under the rule of law.

The issue of equal pay for women was one she addressed in her Human Rights Bills – 'that vexed question of equal pay between men and women',[1] as she called it. She found it deeply unacceptable that women who were doing exactly the same job as men should be paid less than male counterparts. In her election address during her campaign for North Down in the 1969 election, she declared her wish to secure 'equal pay and opportunity for women.' Equal rights for working women was not an election issue for any party in the UK at that time. As with her Human Rights Bills, Sheelagh was ahead of everyone. She defended the right of women to work outside the home – arguing that there was no evidence to show that children of working mothers were damaged – and she supported the setting up of nursery schools, of which there were very few in 1960s. As with other aspects of her human rights campaigns, Sheelagh was influenced in advocating gender equality by events in the United States. Her many visits to the USA had kept her in touch with women's rights activists there. Among them was her cousin, the lawyer Francis Murnaghan.

Francis Murnaghan, during a distinguished career which included 21 years as a federal judge, used 'the Law to realise the American

People's Constitutional Freedoms.'[2] In the 1960s he was 'an early proponent for equality in matters of race and gender', defending civil rights activists – 'At a time when respect for diversity was not yet the norm.'[3] The Murnaghan cousins 'shared a liberal political and philosophy founded on a commitment to protecting and where feasible, extending the rights of marginalised groups in society. Once in a position to promote that philosophy, neither hesitated to act.'[4]

Frank Murnaghan advised Sheelagh when she was drafting her Bills. The 1963 Equal Pay Act in the USA, which sought to outlaw gender discrimination in the workplace, and the Civil Rights Act of 1964, which prohibited discrimination on grounds of gender, were along with similar anti-gender discrimination causes in the Ontario Human Rights Legislation in Canada, used by Sheelagh as blueprints for the legislation which she sought to have enacted in Northern Ireland.

Because Sheelagh's Bills were rejected, it took until the 1970s before laws dealing with equal pay for women made it onto the statute book in Northern Ireland. In 1970, the Equal Pay Act (NI) was passed, in the aftermath of similar legislation in Great Britain. In 1973, the Standing Human Rights Commission included gender equality in its remit. The entry of the UK to the EEC in 1973 was a further impetus towards equality as the Westminster parliament was obliged to pass gender Bills legislation in order to conform to EEC laws and standards. In 1975, the Sex Discrimination Act came into force in Great Britain and this Act was extended to cover Northern Ireland in 1976.

Sheelagh welcomed the Equal Pay Act but shared the concerns expressed at Stormont during the debate on the Bill, by Anne Dickson, who stated: 'The Bill refers to equal pay but does not, I regret to say, refer to equal opportunity or equal salary. Women do not get equal opportunity when it comes to managerial and executive posts.'[5]

The 1976 Sex Discrimination (Northern Ireland) Order created the Equal Opportunities Commission of Northern Ireland (EOCNI), which had powers to investigate individual complaints of discrimination. The Commission did take a proactive approach to discrimination against women in areas such as employment opportunities and pay. But it would be some years before the problem of sexual harassment came up. In the United States, meanwhile, the term 'sexual harassment' had been coined to describe 'unwanted and coercive sexual advances experienced by women at work.' A landmark publication in 1979 by legal academic Catherine McKinnon, *Sexual Harassment of Working Women*, defined two types of harassment. One involved a woman being requested to/expected to provide sexual favours in return for employment and the second type involved situations where 'an employer or co-worker creates a hostile or intimidating work environment for a female employee.'[6]

Sheelagh kept an eye on the ongoing debates on discrimination issues in America and was aware of McKinnon's work. Since 1969, she had also been chairing industrial relations and employment tribunals in Belfast and was working on changing law in the area of employment and equality in Northern Ireland.

In August 1983, after the publication of a Trade Union Congress (TUC) booklet on the problem of sexual harassment in the workplace, the BBC in Northern Ireland did an interview with the Equal Opportunities Commission. EOCNI stated that such harassment 'constituted unlawful sex discrimination.' Soon afterwards a woman who believed herself to have been the victim of such harassment approached EOCNI. The Commission instructed Barrister Noelle McGrenera to take on the case.[7] What would become known as 'M' v Crescent Garage Ltd was heard by the Industrial Relations Tribunal chaired by Sheelagh.[8] Noelle McGrenera recalls Sheelagh as being 'a larger than life character who arrived for the hearing with her dog Brandy, and an adequate supply of cigars for the day.'[9]

The complainant, 'M' had worked as an apprentice garage mechanic. She told the Tribunal how, when she started work, her employer had told her that she was entering 'a man's world' in which she was the only female employee. The Tribunal was told that 'M' had been subjected to months of verbal abuse from the other apprentices, who made it clear to her that they resented her presence. Some of the verbal abuse was of a sexual nature. When she complained to her boss, matters just got worse. Events cumulated in an incident, during the employer's absence on holiday, in which the two mechanics grabbed 'M' by the arms and felt her breasts. She managed to break free but, in doing so, injured her arm and had to wear a sling for a fortnight. She then felt obliged to resign her job.

The two men did not dispute 'M's' version of events but claimed that she was never targeted because she was a woman. Nothing in the

1976 Sex Discrimination Order mentioned sexual harassment specifically, although there were references to discrimination occurring if a female employee were to be treated 'less favourably' than a male employee.[10] 'The hostile work environment definition of sexual harassment had yet to receive general legal acceptance on either side of the Atlantic.'[11] However, despite the lack of case law precedent in the area, Sheelagh had no difficulty in concluding that the Sex Discrimination Act was intended to protect women form this type of workplace abuse. In her ruling, she declared:

> We are aware that it is fairly commonplace for apprentices to be subjected to a certain amount of teasing. But we find on the evidence that the harassment suffered by the applicant went beyond the normal bounds, and had the effect that it became impossible for her to continue her apprenticeship with the respondent. We further find that the main reason for the harassment was the fact that she was a female 'in a man's world', and that it amounted to Sex Discrimination.[12]

The Tribunal ruling also placed blame on the garage manager for his failure to control the two male employees or protect 'M'. Sheelagh awarded the applicant £1,000 in compensation, the highest amount of damages allowed under UK law at the time. Sheelagh's ruling in the case of 'M' v Crescent Garage Ltd set a precedent in the UK and subsequent case law in the area confirmed her original opinion and interpretation of the law. Noelle McGrenera has stated that: 'In making such a finding, Sheelagh Murnaghan paved the way for others in sexual harassment cases within these islands, earning herself a place among the pioneers who have properly influenced society's attitude to women in the workplace generally.'[13]

In 1986, following on from the Crescent Garage case, ECONI published a guide for employers and employees to the problems of sexual harassment entitled, *Sexual Harassment is no Laughing Matter*. It was the first such publication in the United Kingdom. Sexual harassment was made a criminal offence in the UK the same year. Indirectly, Sheelagh's ruling also paved the way for other member states of the European Community to address the harassment issue. In 1985 a Labour Court ruling in the Republic of Ireland reached a nearly identical judgement in a case quite similar to the Crescent

Ulster Liberal group photo early 1970s (left to right):
Colonel Bathoe Rainsford (Press Officer), Mervyn Cowan, Rosemary McGrath,
George Jackson, Brian McGrath, Dorice Jackson, Wallace Perry (Vice-Chairman),
Cecil Bell (Secretary), Brandy (Sheelagh's dog), Jimmy Murray, Sheelagh Murnaghan,
Patricia Cowan (Treasurer), Margaret Goodfellow, Rev. Albert McElroy (President),
Rae Rosenfield, Marie Bell, Phil Wallace, Berkley Farr (Chairman), Peggy Wallace.

Garage case. The Court declared that 'Freedom from Sexual Harassment is a condition of work which an employee of either sex is entitled to expect.'

In 2002, the European Union passed a building directive defining sexual harassment as 'any form of physical conduct of a sexual nature' which has the 'purpose or effect of violating the dignity of a female employee or creating an intimidating, hostile, degrading, humiliating or offensive environment for her/him.' This definition of harassment is now included in the UK sex discrimination laws. Britain and Ireland are somewhat ahead of the rest of the EU in this area of law and that, Constance Rynder believed, was due to Sheelagh:

> That Ireland, Northern Ireland and the UK are finding less difficulty with the new guidelines than are their EU partners owes much to Sheelagh Murnaghan twenty years earlier. She had demonstrated the potential for utilising existing mechanisms to incorporate sexual harassment into the general ban on sex discrimination.[14]

Interestingly, across the Atlantic, Sheelagh's cousin, Judge Frank Murnaghan, was also dealing with sexual harassment cases in his capacity as a Federal Court of Appeals Judge in Baltimore. In 1983, in a case where the court ruled against the plaintiff due to a technicality, Judge Murnaghan wrote a dissenting judgement, in which he stated: 'The majority opinion not only creates a formidable obstacle to an individual plaintiff's quest for vindication of her Civil Rights, but undermines generally the remedial and statutory obligations of Title VII' (of the 1964 Civil Rights Act, outlining discrimination on grounds of colour, creed or gender).

In a 1985 case Judge Murnaghan wrote the majority opinion which invoked the same doctrine which Sheelagh had applied in the Crescent Garage case that a company (or employer) is 'liable for the actions (or, in this case, inaction) of its supervisory personnel in cases of sexual harassment in the workplace.'[15]

Notes

1   Northern Ireland House of Commons Reports, vol. 65, col. 935 (8 Feb. 1966).
2   http://www.murnaghanfellowship.org/judge_murnaghan, accessed 14 May 2019.
3   Ibid.
4   Constance Rynder, 'Sheelagh Murnaghan and the Struggle for Human Rights', *Irish Studies Review*, vol. 14, no. 4 (2006), p. 456.
5   NIHC, vol. 77, cols 634–5 (18 Nov. 1970).
6   Rynder, 'Sheelagh Murnaghan and the Struggle for Human Rights', p. 454.
7   Ibid., p. 455.
8   Ibid.
9   Ibid.
10   Ibid., p. 456.
11   Ibid.
12   Ibid.
13   Ibid.
14   Ibid., p. 457.
15   Ibid., p. 456.

10

Final Years and Legacy

Sheelagh Murnaghan retired from the Tribunal in 1987, although she remained a practising barrister. In the New Year Honours List for 1988 she was awarded the OBE for her services to the community in Northern Ireland and received the award from Queen Elizabeth in Buckingham Palace in the summer. She remained involved with a wide range of community groups and other organisations including the International Federation of Women Lawyers.

The Ulster Liberal Party continued to decline through the late 1970s. Attempts at a party re-launch in 1976 were unsuccessful and in the 1979 elections to the European parliament, the Liberal candidate for Northern Ireland received only 0.1 per cent of the vote in what was a low poll.[1] The last time the party contested an election was in the 1985 district council elections. The Ulster Liberals ceased to exist as an autonomous entity in 1987.[2] Sheelagh did not miss her political career greatly and would not have resumed it. In her last years she became increasingly interested in environmental issues.[3] She never married and appears to have had no relationships. Fr Alec Reid described her as a person who 'never gave herself the chance to be loved.'[4]

She remained throughout her adult life the 'linchpin' of her large family. After the death of her father in 1964, she looked after her mother until her death in 1967. Siblings and later nieces and nephews stayed at her Belfast home while attending college and sometimes received financial support from her. Although she did not often take holidays, she visited family and other relatives in America, Canada and elsewhere. She also moved to a rural home in County Down near Crossgar. She had a great love for dogs and owned a number of them.

Sheelagh did not live to see the beginning of the Peace Process and the end of the Troubles. She died from cancer on 14 September 1993, aged 69. The funeral Mass in Belfast was taken by her good friend Fr Alec Reid. Tributes to her appeared in the Irish and British press – including appreciations from Maurice Hayes, Jeremy Thorpe and from her nephew, the TV broadcaster Dermot Murnaghan.

The Legacy

Sheelagh once told Maurice Hayes that: 'Nobody could have a greater sense of failure that I have.' She was, perhaps, too harsh on herself. It was certainly the case that she could not persuade the government of the day to accept her Human Rights bills or the complete abolition of the death penalty, but much of what she campaigned for did come to pass within a few years: power-sharing government and a PR voting system, an ombudsman for Northern Ireland, reform of the police, fair employment acts, equal pay laws.

Her ruling in the 'M' v Crescent Garage Ltd case helped make sexual harassment in the workplace a criminal offence in the United Kingdom. In 1998 the UK government introduced the Human Rights Act which incorporated the European Convention on Human Rights into British law. During a debate on a Human Rights Bill in the House of Lords in 1997, the former Alliance Party leader John Alderdice recalled how 31 years almost to the day earlier, Sheelagh had introduced her second Human Rights Bill in Stormont. Alderdice referred to Sheelagh as 'the Helen Suzman of Northern Ireland – a substantial lady in her principles and politics.'[5]

When she put forward her human rights bills, she was the first to do so in Northern Ireland or any other part of the UK. Few paid heed to her then and that was to be Northern Ireland's tragedy. Within a decade, however, all political parties were publicly advocating the need for some kind of Bill of Rights/Human Rights legislation. At the 1996 Northern Ireland Forum there was agreement among all the ten political groups represented that there should be a Bill of Rights for Northern Ireland.

The Good Friday/Belfast Agreement embodied much of what Sheelagh had tried to achieve for her country – not just the power-sharing and the PR voting system, but the principles of mutual respect for diversity and different identities and political views contained in the document. Mary Robinson – then the United Nations High Commissioner for Human Rights – stated that the Agreement was 'conspicuous by the centrality it gives to Equality and Human Rights concerns.'[6] *The Guardian* newspaper also noted that aspect 'Equality and Human Rights infuses the whole document.'[7]

Constance Rynder wrote in 2006 that after the collapse of the Sunningdale Agreement in 1974:

> Twenty more years of communal conflict ensued, however, before Sheelagh Murnaghan's Human Rights agenda would find its way back into the national debate. That it ultimately did owed much to a new generation of women activists absolutely committed to a Bill of Rights for Northern Ireland.[8]

Among these new activists was Dr Monica McWilliams, co-founder and leader of the Northern Ireland Women's Coalition. According to Rynder, Dr McWilliams acknowledged the debt her party owed to Sheelagh's pioneering efforts on behalf of Human Rights legislation. The Good Friday Agreement mandated the establishment of a new Northern Ireland Human Rights Commission and this came into existence in March 1999. The Commission published its recommendations in September 2001, which called for specific protection for the rights of women and minorities. The resulting debate in the Northern Ireland Assembly was the first occasion on which Human Rights was debated in a Northern Ireland legislature since Sheelagh's fourth Bill in January 1968. The debate was frequently a bitter one, echoing the 'entrenched attitudes of the past, on both sides',[9] which Sheelagh had so deplored, voiced by many. Some Unionists accused the Human Rights Commission of 'bias' against Protestants and Unionists. Mary Nelis, a Sinn Féin MLA, responded to this:

> This is not the first time that Unionism has dismissed efforts to enact a Bill of Rights here. When the late Sheelagh Murnaghan tried to do so in the 1960s her efforts were stonewalled by the same Unionist mindset that is on display here. In retrospect, those Unionists might reflect that, had they placed a Bill of Rights on the political agenda then, this society might have been spared 30 years of conflict.[10]

The suspension of devolved government between 2002 and 2007, and afterwards funding shortages delayed the introduction of a Bill of Rights. On 16 June 2005 – 41 years to the day after Sheelagh's first

Human Rights Bill was debated and rejected, Monica McWilliams was appointed as Chief Commissioner of the Northern Ireland Human Rights Commission. As Constance Rynder wrote in 2006, Dr McWilliams 'outlined her Commission's strategy for achieving what eluded Sheelagh Murnaghan in the 1960s, the SACHR in the 1970/80s and the post Good Friday Agreement NIHRC'. Like Sheelagh before her, Dr McWilliams found it extraordinary that, 'The minimum standards set out in the European Convention as the benchmark for a modern democracy are still resented, contested and subject to derogations and restrictive interpretations.' Again writing in 2006, Constance Rynder stated:

> It remains to be seen whether a new generation of Northern Ireland policy makers, led by a latter day Sheelagh Murnaghan, can complete what began over 40 years earlier with a private members Bill on the floor of the old Stormont House of Commons.[11]

In May 2007 devolved government returned to Northern Ireland under the leadership of Ian Paisley and Martin McGuinness. The issue of a Bill of Rights again came under consideration. During a debate in the Assembly in October 2007, an Alliance Party MLA, Stephen Farry noted: '… we have been discussing a Bill of Rights for Northern Ireland since as far back as 1964, when Sheelagh Murnaghan proposed a Motion on this subject in this Chamber.'[12]

A decade further on and Northern Ireland still lacks a Bill of Rights. Issues of equality and human rights such as an Irish Language Act, gay marriage and abortion rights continue to divide the community and were a factor in the collapse of the Stormont government. Brexit has added new complications to the protection of Northern Irish citizens under European Human Rights laws. Sectarianism and other forms of prejudice have not gone away. Nevertheless, there has been progress. Discrimination against people on grounds of race, creed, disability, sexual orientation, disability and political opinion is illegal and so is sexual harassment. The Traveller community, for whose welfare Sheelagh so long campaigned, are now recognised as an ethnic minority. The number of women in the political and legal professions (many of them Catholic) has grown considerably. As Sheelagh had foreseen, Northern Ireland has become a more ethnically diverse society. There are no longer degrees of citizenship in the way that there were when Sheelagh was in political life. The real remedies she sought for those who felt themselves to be victims of injustice are firmly established and there are many of them.

Sheelagh Murnaghan, politician, lawyer, community activist and sportswoman, overcame the problems of being a woman, a Liberal and a Catholic in Northern Ireland. Throughout her life she was a passionate defender of all those who were denied equality. She was a patriot who loved her country and wanted the best for it. She deserves to be remembered and honoured.

Notes

1   The Ulster Liberal candidate for the 1979 European elections was
        James Murray, a schoolteacher from County Down.
2   Gordon Gillespie, 'The Ulster Liberal Party 1956–1973',
        MSSc thesis (Queen's University Belfast, 1984), p. 82.
3   Interview with Lucille McGinley, 2 Aug. 2017.
4   Interview with Fr Alec Reid by Nick McGinley, (nephew of Sheelagh
        Murnaghan) DVD (2004).
5   https://api.parliament.uk/historic-hansard/lords/1997/feb/05/
        human-rights-bill-hl (col. 1742), accessed 14 May 2019.
6   Anne Smith, Monica McWilliams and Primayarda Yarnell, *Political
        Capacity Building: Advancing a Bill of Rights for Northern Ireland*
        (Belfast, 2014), p. 24.
7   *The Guardian*, 11 Apr. 1998.
8   Constance Rynder, 'Sheelagh Murnaghan and the Struggle for Human
        Rights', *Irish Studies Review*, vol. 14, no. 4 (2006), p. 452.
9   Ibid.
10 http://archive.niassembly.gov.uk/record/reports/010925c.htm,
        accessed 14 May 2019.
11 Rynder, 'Sheelagh Murnaghan and the Struggle for Human Rights',
        p. 454.
12 http://archive.niassembly.gov.uk/record/reports2007/071015.htm#3,
        accessed 14 May 2019.

Northern Ireland Assembly Election

JUNE 28, 1973

South Belfast constituency

L
I
B
E
R
A
L

Sheelagh Murnaghan ∎

FIRST PREFERENCE FOR SANITY.

WOMEN! Do you want your Children to be fountains of hate?

YOUNG PEOPLE! Do you want to inherit a desert?

Give your answer by voting
No. 1 FOR SHEELAGH MURNAGHAN.
Your vote will not be wasted.
NORTHERN IRELAND NEEDS POLITICIANS WHO ARE MORE SEEN THAN HEARD

If elected, Sheelagh Murnaghan will be seen in every street, in every home, where people need her help.

GOOD CAN DEFEAT EVIL

NOTHING ELSE CAN

VIOLENCE IS WRONG

HATRED IS OBSCENE

NORTHERN IRELAND IS IN THE GRIP OF A TERRIBLE EVIL

No cause, however sincere, could justify the kind of deeds which have been done here. No cause, whether it be the unification of Ireland or the preservation of Ulster, is furthered by opening the flood gates of evil. Mangled bodies and distorted minds will haunt the years ahead.

We cannot undo what has been done. We can, if we are determined enough, and have faith enough, replace this boiling madness with the cool clear light of reason.

NO MIRACLE CAN BE ACHIEVED OVERNIGHT

VIOLENCE DOES NOT GO OUT LIKE A CANDLE

HATRED CANNOT BE TURNED OFF LIKE A TAP

WE MUST NOT BE DISHEARTENED

VIOLENCE IS WRONG

1973 South Belfast election address and poster for NI Assembly
(PRONI, D230/8/3/10)

Appendix 1
Equality and Anti-Discrimination Legislation
in Northern Ireland
1969–2017

1969   Parliamentary Commissioner Act (NI)
       Established an Ombudsman Office for first time in Northern
       Ireland.

1969   Commissioner for Complaints Act (NI)

1970   Equal Pay Act (NI)

1970   Prevention of Incitement to Hatred Act (NI)

1971   Housing Executive Act (NI)

1973   Standing Advisory Commission on Human Rights set up as part
       of the Northern Ireland Constitution Act.

1973   NI (Emergency Provisions) Act
       Abolished capital punishment for murder in Northern Ireland.

1976   Sex Discrimination (NI) Order
       The Equality Opportunities Commission for Northern Ireland
       (ECONI) was set up to monitor the workings of this order.

1976   Fair Employment (NI) Order
       The Fair Employment Agency was formed to monitor the
       workings of this Act.

1982   Homosexual Offences (NI) Order
       This decriminalised homosexuality in Northern Ireland.

1989   Fair Employment Commission set up to replace the Fair
       Employment Agency and acquired greater powers.

1995   Disability Discrimination Act

1996   Ombudsman (NI) Order

1996   Commissioner for Complaints (NI) Order
       Under this Act the Commissioner was renamed the Assembly
       Ombudsman for Northern Ireland and his/her jurisdiction was
       extended to the investigation of complaints where a person
       aggrieved 'has exercised his rights before a Tribunal but
       complains that injustice remains unremedied.'

1997   Protection from Harassment (NI) Order

1997   Race Relations (NI) Order
       This prohibited discrimination on grounds of colour,
       nationality or ethnic/national origin. Travellers were covered by
       the legislation as an ethnic minority.

1998   Good Friday/Belfast Agreement
       Article 75 of the Agreement requires public bodies to have due
       regard to promote equality between people on grounds of
       religious belief, political opinion, race, age, marital status, sexual
       orientation, disability and gender.

1998   Human Rights Act
       This Act incorporated the European Convention on Human
       Rights into UK law.

1998   Fair Employment and Treatment (NI) Order

1998   UK Parliament abolishes capital punishment for treason.

1999   Northern Ireland Human Rights Commission (NICRA) set up
       under terms of the Good Friday/Belfast Agreement.

2000   Equality (Disability) NI Order

2001   Sex Discrimination (Indirect Discrimination) Regulations (NI)

2001   Special Education Needs and Disability Act

2003   Employment Equality (Sexual Orientation) Regulations (NI)

2003   UK accedes to 13th Protocol of The European Human Rights
       Convention on the complete abolition of the death penalty.

2004   Gender Recognition Act

2004   Civil Partnership Act
       This Act legalised civil partnerships between same sex couples.
       The first civil partnership ceremony in the United Kingdom
       took place in Belfast in 2005.

2006   Employment Equality (Age) Act

2006   Disability Discrimination (NI) Order

2006   Equality Act

2009   Disability Discrimination (Transport) Regulations (NI) Act

2011   Autism Act (NI)
       This Act extends anti-discrimination law protections to those
       on the autism spectrum.

2016   Justice Act (NI)
       This Act set up the Office of Prison Ombudsman.

Appendix 2
Women Members
of the Northern Ireland Parliament
1921–72

Dame Dehra Parker OBE

Party:	Ulster Unionist	
Constituency:	Londonderry City and County	1921–9
	Londonderry South	1933–60
Appointments:	Parliamentary Secretary, Ministry of Education	1937–44
	Minister for Health and Local Government	1949–57

Julie McMordie OBE

Party:	Ulster Unionist	
Constituency:	Belfast South	1921–5
Appointments:	First woman member of Belfast City Council	1919
	First woman High Sheriff of Belfast	1928

Margaret Waring CBE

Party:	Ulster Unionist	
Constituency:	Iveagh	1929–33

Lilian Calvert

Party:	Ulster Unionist	
Constituency:	Queen's University	1944–53

Dinah McNabb

Party:	Ulster Unionist	
Constituency:	Armagh North	1945–69

Dr Eileen Hickey
Party: Independent
Constituency: Queen's University   1949–58

Bessie Maconachie
Party: Ulster Unionist
Constituency: Queen's University   1953–69

Sheelagh Murnaghan OBE
Party: Ulster Liberal
Constituency: Queen's University   1961–9

Anne Dickson
Party: Ulster Unionist
Constituency: Carrick   1969–72

Appointments: First woman to lead a political party
                in Northern Ireland.
              Leader of the Unionist Party
                of Northern Ireland (UPNI)   1976–81

SENATE

Marian Greeves MBE
Party: Independent
Served: 1950–58

Edith Taggart
Party: Ulster Unionist
Served: 1950–58

Appendix 3
'Ballad of Human Rights'

Following the failure of Sheelagh's second Human Rights Bill in February 1966, a ballad was written about the parliamentary debate and the rejection of the bill.

"Twas on the eighth of Febru'ry
In Stormont's halls proceeding
That Sheelagh's Bill for Human Rights
Came up for second reading.
MPs assembled, bringing all
Their dash and verve and go,
The Unionists determined to
Preserve the status quo.

Plain speaking came from Stewart and Fitt
And Diamond, Boyd and Currie:
The incidents they mentioned should
Have made the members worry,
But Bradford swept them all aside
By saying Human Rights
Might interfere with liberty
And lead to human fights;

And John D. Taylor's maiden speech
Did not assist us much;
He thought those who complained were just
A little out of touch;
He thought that nothing should be done
In case we came a cropper.
To make a sin illegal – well,
It was not right and proper.

Phelim O'Neill was in a fix.
He did not want to shirk.
He liked the Bill in principle
But feared it would not work.
He read it o'er and o'er again,
His conscience racked and strained.
He wondered what on earth to do
And in the end abstained.

The Minister for Home Affairs
With governmental weight
Rose up, all dapper and assured,
To answer the debate.
Miss Murnaghan, he thought, should cease
Her annual agitation,
Though he deplored – he did indeed –
This thing discrimination.

The Unionist backbenchers yawned
And wished she'd go away.
They threw it out the time before –
Why bring it back today?
Why keep insisting stubbornly
On awkward things like rights?
We're doing fine the way we are
So let us sleep o' nights.

The Government of Ireland Act
Is all we really need
For it forbids all laws against
A man because of creed;
And as for other things, if there's
A tendency to bias
In housing and employment, say,
Such things are sent to try us.

So Sheelagh's Bill was voted down,
Once more with smugness greeted,
But she will go to Westminster;
She will not be defeated,

And when she does the Big Ben chimes
Will mock those who insist
That they can cure a social ill
By saying "It don't exist."

LIBRA

Published by the Ulster Liberal Association,
Brook House, Newtownards.

Appendix 4
First Roman Catholic/Female Senior Political and Legal Office Holders in Northern Ireland 1921–2017

1921   Sir Denis Henry QC, a Roman Catholic Unionist, appointed first Lord Chief Justice of Northern Ireland.

1938   Dehra Parker MP becomes the first woman to serve in a Northern Ireland government when she is appointed Parliamentary Secretary at the Department of Education.

1949   Dame Dehra Parker MP becomes the first female Cabinet Minister in a Northern Ireland government. She serves as Minister for Health until 1957. She is also the first woman to be appointed to the Privy Council of Northern Ireland.

1970   South African-born Claire Palley becomes Professor of Law and Dean of the School of Law at Queen's University Belfast. She is the first female Professor of Law in the United Kingdom.

1971   Gerald Newe becomes the first Catholic to serve in a Northern Ireland government when he is appointed as Minister for Community Relations.

1972   Following the imposition of direct rule, the Attorney-General for England and Wales, Sir Peter Rawlinson QC, MP, also becomes Attorney-General for Northern Ireland. He is the first Catholic to hold the post.

1973   Sir James Flanagan is appointed as the first Catholic Chief Constable of the RUC.

1976   Anne Dickson is elected leader of the Unionist Party of
       Northern Ireland (UPNI). She is the first woman to lead a
       Northern Ireland political party.

1977   Maurice Hayes becomes the first Catholic Ombudsman for
       Northern Ireland.

1978   Barbara Calvert from England becomes the first female QC
       called to the Northern Ireland Bar. Eilis McDermott will later
       become the first Northern Irish-born female QC.

1979   Margaret Thatcher MP becomes the first female Prime Minister
       of the United Kingdom of Great Britain and Northern Ireland.

1982   Grace Bannister becomes the first female Lord Mayor of Belfast.

1991   Jill McIvor appointed as the first female Ombudsman of
       Northern Ireland.

1997   Dr Mo Mowlam MP becomes the first female Northern Ireland
       Secretary.

1997   Mary McAleese becomes the first Northern Ireland-born
       President of Ireland.

1998   Corinne Philpott QC becomes the first female County Court
       Judge in Northern Ireland.

1999   Bairbre De Brún (SF) and Brid Rodgers (SDLP) become the
       first Catholic women to serve in a Northern Ireland government.

2001   John Reid MP becomes the first Catholic Secretary of State for
       Northern Ireland.

2007   Baroness Patricia Scotland QC becomes the first female
       Attorney-General of England, Wales and Northern Ireland. A
       Catholic, she is also the first black Attorney General.

2007   Dawn Purvis becomes first female leader of the Progressive
       Unionist Party.

2010   Following the restoration of justice powers to the Northern
       Ireland Executive, John Larkin QC becomes the first Northern
       Irish-born Catholic to hold the office of Attorney General for
       Northern Ireland.

2010   Margaret Ritchie becomes the first female leader of the SDLP.

2011   Barra McGrory becomes the first Catholic Director of Public
       Prosecutions (DPP) for Northern Ireland.

2015   Denise McBride QC and Siobhan Keegan QC are appointed as
       the first women High Court judges in Northern Ireland.

2016   Arlene Foster MLA becomes the first female First Minister of
       Northern Ireland and the first woman leader of the
       Democratic Unionist Party.

2016   Naomi Long MLA becomes the first woman to lead the Alliance
       Party.

2016   Claire Sugden becomes the first female Justice Minister in
       Northern Ireland.

2017   Lady Justice Brenda Hale becomes the first female President of
       the United Kingdom Supreme Court.

Bibliography

PUBLISHED

Books

Jonathan Bardon, *A History of Ulster* (Belfast, 1992).

Brice Dickson, *The European Convention of Human Rights and the Conflict in Northern Ireland* (Oxford, 2010).

Gordon Gillespie, *Albert McElroy: The Radical Minister 1915–1975* (Belfast, 1985).

Omer Grech, *Human Rights and The Northern Ireland Conflict: Law, Politics and Conflict, 1921–2014* (Oxford, 2017).

Maurice Hayes, *Minority Verdict: Experiences of a Catholic Civil Servant* (Belfast, 1995).

Myrtle Hill, *Women in Ireland: A Century of Change,* (Belfast, 2003).

Michael Kennedy, *Divisions and Consensus: The Politics of Cross-Border Relations, 1925–1969* (Dublin, 2000).

Conn McCluskey, *Up off their Knees: A Commentary on the Civil Rights Movement in Northern Ireland* (Dublin, 1989).

James McGuire and James Quinn (eds), *Dictionary of Irish Biography*, 9 vols (Cambridge, 2009).

Meadbh McNamara and Paschal Mooney, *Women in Parliament Ireland 1918–2000* (Dublin, 2000).

Monica McWilliams, Anne Smyth and Priyamvada Yarnell, *Political Capacity Building: Advancing a Bill of Rights for Northern Ireland* (Belfast, 2014).

Sheila Rowbotham, *A Century of Women* (London, 1997).

Journal articles

Berkley Farr, 'Liberalism in Unionist Northern Ireland', *Journal of Liberal Democrat History*, no. 33 (Winter 2000/01).

Constance Rynder, 'Sheelagh Murnaghan and the Struggle for Human Rights in Northern Ireland', *Irish Studies Review*, vol. 14, no. 4 (2006).

Constance Rynder, 'Sheelagh Murnaghan and the Ulster Liberal Party', *Journal of Liberal History*, vol. 7 (Summer 2011).

Newspapers

Belfast Telegraph
The Guardian
Irish Independent
Irish Press
The Irish Times
Ulster Herald
Westmeath Independent

Publications of political parties

Northern Radical (1966–76)

UNPUBLISHED

Barkley Farr, personal papers.
Gordon Gillespie, 'The Ulster Liberal Party 1956–1973', MSSc. thesis (Queen's University Belfast, 1984).
Ulster Liberal Party Papers 1960–73, PRONI D2591 (see also D3342).
Chaminda Weerawardhana, 'The Wise Doctor of Ulster's Ills: Revisiting the Legacy of Sheelagh Murnaghan LLB, MP, OBE', paper presented Queen's University Belfast, 24 Mar. 2017.

DVD

'"Sheelagh Murnaghan": Interviews with Fr Alec Reid and Dr Maurice Hayes', by Nick McGinley (2004).

PARLIAMENTARY RECORDS

Northern Ireland House of Commons Reports, 1961–9.

Index